Mountain Folk

Lynn Coffey

Copyright © 2015
by Lynn Coffey
All rights reserved, including the right to reproduce this
work in any form whatsoever, without permission
in writing from the author, except for brief passages
in connection with a review.

Cover design by Jane Hagaman
Front cover photo: © Robert Benson of Raphine, Virginia (Stanley Garfield Cash
    and wife, Littie Bell Mays Cash, of Cashtown, Virginia, 1965)
Back cover photo: © Lynn Coffey (Robert and Bobby Henderson and Junior Rhodes
    at Love, Virginia, December 1987)
Photo of Back Creek: © Vanessa Fraser of Love, Virginia
Author photograph: © Rebecca Coffey Thompson
Interior design by Jane Hagaman
All current interior photographs by Lynn Coffey
Vintage family photos in each chapter courtesy of those interviewed

All the information in the interviews is as told to Lynn Coffey. The
author is not responsible for any misinformation.

Quartet Books
Charlottesville, VA
www.quartetbooks.com

If you are unable to order this book from your local
bookseller, you may order directly from the author.
Call (540) 949-0329 or use the order form in the back
of the book. For more information about this book or
the Backroads series of books, you may browse Lynn's
website at www.backroadsbooks.com.

Library of Congress Control Number: 2015905034

ISBN 978-0-692-40291-7
10 9 8 7 6 5 4 3 2 1
Printed on acid-free paper in the United States

This book is dedicated to Owen Garfield Campbell.

On the dedication page of all four of my previous books, I chose a photograph that was dear to my heart and included a short inscription above it. *Mountain Folk* differs, in that there is a story to go along with the photo, and that story is the first you'll read.

ALSO BY LYNN COFFEY

Backroads 1: Plain Folk and Simple Livin'
Backroads 2: The Road to Chicken Holler
Backroads 3: Faces of Appalachia
Appalachian Heart

(All books are available from the author's website:
www.backroadsbooks.com)

Contents

Dedication Story ix
Foreword, by Ted Hughes xvii
Acknowledgments xix
Introduction xxi

1. Ruby May Cook Henderson 1
2. Ronald Massie "Butch" Taylor 17
3. Audrey Carol Campbell Smegal 33
4. Kenneth Ray Fitzgerald 51
5. Frances May Hudson Fitzgerald 65
6. Marvin Samuel Henderson 81
7. The Fitzgerald Sisters 99
   Peggy Ballowe and Barbara Gormes
8. Irma Marshall Bowling Roberts 119
9. Martin Samuel "Buddy" Truslow 137
10. Betty Marie Bryant Roberts 155
11. Carl Franklin Coffey 169
12. Sarah Jane Hatter Urbanski 189
13. William Harrison Thompson, Jr. 207
14. Doris Elizabeth Brooks Bryant 227
15. Loyd Dale Ogden, Sr. 241
16. Maybell "Mabel" Frances Truslow Napier 261
Poem: Back Creek 281

Dedication Story

Owen Garfield Campbell passed away on Tuesday, January 14, 2014, and with his death came another significant loss, besides the aching hearts of those who loved him. Owen was one of the last true mountain men in our area. Born into an era before most modern conveniences, he chose to continue living the same way his ancestors had hundreds of years before; without electricity or indoor plumbing or even a vehicle, preferring to walk the mountains he knew like the back of his hand. He was the genuine article. And there lies the loss, not only Owen's passing but the death of a way of life that is all but gone and few can remember.

When Owen left this world, bound for the eternal heaven he believed in, he had little in the way of personal possessions: a shotgun, a bed, and a small shaving mirror. But what he lacked in material goods, he made up for in a rich legacy of living that can never be duplicated.

I met Owen back in the 1980s while covering stories and taking pictures for *Backroads* newspaper. I still have the photo of him standing next to Ralph and Luther Cash and Freddie Seaman at the State Fish Hatchery in Montebello, where he was visiting that day. At the time, I didn't know him personally, but it wasn't too long afterward that Margie Hatter invited me to come with her and several others up to the old Averill Campbell graveyard, high on the mountain near Spy Rock.

It was there that I was formally introduced to Owen (or "Owens," as the locals called him), standing among the tombstones of Campbell and Cash family members. The old cemetery had an ethereal quality to it, shaded by huge oaks, wild ferns and periwinkle carpeting the ground. I snapped a picture of Owen talking with Margie, his arm draped across the weathered fence surrounding the cemetery, and it became one of my favorites. It was in the fall, and he was wearing his standard bib overalls, worn denim coat, and faded Carhartt hat with the ear flaps turned down.

He was sporting the ever-present toothless grin that lit up his face and made you want to engage him in conversation. The deep creases around his kind eyes told of years of humor and the gentle disposition for which he was known. I framed the picture, and it hangs on my office wall with so many other photos of the mountain people. I chose that particular picture for the front cover of my third book, *Faces of Appalachia*, because, as they say, a picture is worth a thousand words. Owen truly *was* the face of Appalachia.

Two dear friends, Lowell and Viola Humphreys, grew up with Owen and had much to say about the man to whom this book is dedicated. I thank them for their memories, as well as this priceless information that has turned out to be Owen's eulogy.

Owen's grandparents on his father's side were Lewis and Millie Massie Campbell. On the maternal side were Stanley and Littie Bell Mays Cash (photo on the front cover). Owen's parents were Matthew, whom they called "Matha," and Annie Cash Campbell. Owen was the eldest of their three children, born June 16, 1923, at the foot of the mountain near Piney River.

In the early 1940s, Matthew purchased 297 acres, known as the Averill Campbell place, in the shadow of Spy Rock; the family moved there when Owen was around twenty years old. It is where he lived his entire adult life, other than the last few years when his health declined, and he became a resident of Ruxton nursing facility in Staunton. Lowell said that while visiting the nursing home, Owen told him that they cooked different foods there, and it was hard to get used to them. He was used to eating "rough vittles," as he called them, meaning brown beans, cabbage, and the cornbread he was raised on.

As a young man, Owen worked with his daddy, cutting extract wood with crosscut saws; while his brother, Jimmy, did the same type of work with his mother. Their sister, Maybelle, worked around the home, doing housework, milking cows, cooking, and tending the garden.

Owen had a tendency to stay back in the mountains, but Lowell said that after Owen became the off-bearer at Billy Byers's sawmill, they saw more of him. Lowell remembers that in the early 1980s, Owen had an accident.

"Owens fell out of a tree and got all broke up. He was shaking apples out of a tree in the hog lot when he lost his balance and fell on an old snag that had been sawed off in the lot. He broke his pelvis and his arm, and Jimmy hauled him back to the house in a wheelbarrow. He stayed in Waynesboro Hospital for I don't know how many weeks, in traction, and he'd tell them to read the Bible to him. The doctors said he would never be able to work again, but right after that, he went back to being the slab off-bearer at the sawmill."

The family attended Mount Paran Baptist Church and always came to the annual homecoming service, and, Lowell added, "Back then there was two weeks of revival, and I remember the family would come every night and walk home in the dark with lanterns or flashlights, if nobody took them [home by car]."

Lowell also said of Owen, "He was raised to get up early (3:30 a.m.) to do chores, such as feeding and watering his horse. He plowed the garden with the horse and could cook a little, too, often stopping to make a pone of cornbread, as he called it. He could play a little on the guitar, and his daddy could play the banjo. Matha played a lot at dances when he was younger, before he got married.

"We went over there one day not many years before Mr. Campbell passed away—he died in 1980—and he had a banjo with a groundhog hide stretched across the front. It had no back on it. Mr. Campbell played the old time claw-hammer style, like Grandpa Jones, and he played good even as an old man. He knew all the old songs. They just took up playing music. Nobody showed them how to play; the music was just in them."

Owen had an easygoing, gentle personality, humble and meek but with much good humor. If he got excited about something he was talking about, Owen's voice would go up about three octaves, and I never tired of listening to his high-pitched, musical conversation. Lowell said that he had many of the mannerisms of his grandfather, Stanley Cash, and reminded him of the man.

"[Owen] looked a lot like him, and [Stanley] was always doing something; [he] was never still. And I never heard [Owen] cuss in my life. Never! He told me, 'Mammy broke me from that. If Mammy get ahold of some of those kids now, she'd would teach them not to say those words!'"

Lowell said that the old mountain people referred to dirty words or cussing as "blackguard."

Viola said that when she and Lowell were the farm managers at Skylark Farm on the Blue Ridge Parkway, Owen often came out to spend the weekend with them. Lowell said that Owen also worked there laying rock, putting up drywall, or helping to do some fencing and mowing. Viola would give him a haircut or wash his clothes when the day's work was done.

This says a lot about trust, and Viola wisely commented, "It's all about knowing how to approach a person when you are doing personal things for them. Owen was always so appreciative for anything you'd do for him."

Lowell added, "You don't want to push nothing on the mountain people; they've got a mind of their own."

Lowell and Owen did a lot of hunting and fishing together over the years, and Lowell said that Owen was the best at finding a little worm called a "pennywinkle" that the trout loved. He was also a patient fisherman. "If a native trout was in a hole of water, he'd fish for a half hour until he finally caught him." On hunting, Lowell said that Owen mostly shot squirrels. "He didn't want to hunt deer or bear, and deer weren't as plentiful back then like they are now. He shot a few bear to make them get out of his way when he was squirrel hunting!"

Owen had a very strong faith in God and was quick to tell anyone who didn't believe or was not living the kind of life he thought a Christian should live that, if they didn't make things right before they died, "My preacher, Billy Coffey, says you are going to go to hell!"

Owen never married, although Lowell said that if he had gotten out in the world more and met people, he would have made a good husband for any woman. Asked if there was anything else special about Owen, Viola said that he loved children. "He'd come and watch cartoons on TV with our son, L. E., and would play with him just like a child. L. E. would climb up in his lap and talk to him, and Owen, in turn, would answer him back in a childlike voice, and they would have the best conversation."

As we wound up our own conversation, I asked if there was anything else they would like to say about Owen, and Lowell said, "He was a great guy and going to be really missed. You never heard anyone say anything bad about Owens. He was a worker . . . never knew nothing but hard work."

Viola smiled and said, "The thing that was so beautiful at the end was that Owens found someone who truly, truly loved him."

He'd met Alma, who was also a resident at Ruxton, and they'd had a very special relationship while living there. And that's all anyone can hope for: to give and to receive love that comes from the heart.

So I'd like to dedicate this book about the Appalachian people and their way of life to a man who represented the culture in its truest form: Owen Garfield Campbell.

Phillip Greene, Tyro, Virginia

Ted Hughes (1951–2015)

Foreword

Once again, Lynn Coffey brings the stories and tales of the Blue Ridge Mountain people to life. Lynn's passion and dedication to preserving the history of these people's lives and "mountain ways" will be a work that researchers and historians will find invaluable now and for generations to come.

In her fifth book, *Mountain Folk*, Lynn continues her interviews with the people of the Blue Ridge she admires and treasures so much. She insists that the gift she has in writing about these native folk is a gift from God; she is merely the "vessel" to carry forward the stories the people give to her.

Lynn's passion for learning as much as she can about the mountain people and their culture has never faltered or waned. She still gets just as excited today as she did thirty years ago to learn something about the old ways.

Lynn Coffey is not only a writer and photographer but also has had hands-on experience with the daily chores of living she writes about. Whether it is herding cattle, butchering hogs, making apple butter, digging ginseng, hunting squirrels, or playing the spoons, Lynn has been a student of mountain life. Now Lynn has become the teacher!

From material and anecdotes she has collected over the years, Lynn truly understands that everyone has a story to share. Her gentle nature and genuine concern about the preservation of mountain life is reflected in her heartfelt writing style.

Join Lynn again as she travels the back roads, discovering new treasures from the people who call the Blue Ridge Mountains home.

—Ted Hughes
October 21, 2014

NOTE: Ted Hughes, my dear friend of thirty-five years, died in April 2015. For many years, he and his wife, Noel, lived in Stuarts Draft, Virginia, where Noel continues to make her home. Ted consulted on several books and articles concerning life in the Blue Ridge Mountains. He retired from the University of Virginia, then worked for eleven years as an interpretative ranger on the Blue Ridge Parkway. He will be greatly missed.

Acknowledgments

While my name is on the front cover as the author, I am just the one putting the stories together and getting it ready for print. There are many others responsible for making this book possible, thus preserving a bit of early history from where I live: the Blue Ridge Mountains.

First and foremost, I thank God for giving me the gift of being able to write and take photographs and sending me to an area where both could be used to capture a culture that is slowly ebbing away. He instilled in me at an early age the desire to know more about the "old ways," then plopped me down right into the midst of the people who could teach me how to live that way. He took an average housewife with no prior experience and somehow made her into a spokesman for the mountain people. Give God the credit; I am just his vessel.

Second, I thank my long-suffering husband, Billy, for putting up with a wife who is obsessed with writing down stories from centuries of which she was never a part. How fitting that I've done this for long enough to now be the same age as the people I've interviewed for *Mountain Folk*! Billy is the one who figures out what needs to be done on the computer, then patiently does it amid tiny lectures on how I need to learn to do it for myself. His question, "What's going to happen if something happens to me?" is always answered, "That's when I'll quit." Pray for his good health!

I thank Robert Benson, of Raphine, for sending me a photograph he took in 1965. He was walking through the mountains where Stanley and Littie Bell Mays Cash lived and asked if he could snap their picture. Although he didn't know them, something clicked for me when he told me that they lived in a remote area behind Crabtree Falls. I realized they were the grandparents of Frances and Mary Cash, whose photo is on the back cover of *Appalachian Heart*. When I saw the photo, the idea for another book popped in my head, and I asked Robert's permission to use his picture as the front cover for this book. Littie Bell Mays Cash was born September 29, 1882, and died April 28, 1970. Stanley Garfield Cash was born October 7, 1876, and died one month after his wife on May 29, 1970.

I must give a huge amount of credit to the girls of Quartet Books: Tania Seymour, Jane Hagaman, Cynthia Mitchell, and Sara Sgarlat. We started out as fledglings in 2008; they, forming their own company to help new authors self-publish their work, and I, their first customer. The result of that chance meeting was my first book, *Backroads: Plain Folk and Simple Livin'*, which came out in the fall of 2009. It was so successful that I decided to stick with them for four consecutive books, and they have never disappointed me.

My most important thank you goes to the mountain people themselves, who allowed an "outsider" to write their stories for more than thirty years and adopted me into their families as one of their own. You have filled my heart with untold joy and given me enough precious memories to last a lifetime.

Introduction

Everyone has a story. I have always gravitated toward people whose stories have never been documented. By the world's standards, most of us are not Pulitzer Prize winners; but in God's eyes, no one is more important than another. We are all pieces of a gigantic mosaic in which every single person adds to the whole, making a beautiful picture of mankind. My contribution to the mosaic seems to be recording the lives of everyday people who were brought up during an era far different from what we know today. I started out talking to grandparents and parents; now in *Mountain Folk*, I am talking to the children of those early mountain pioneers.

Proverbs 1:5 says, "Let the wise listen and add to their learning." My prayer for each person reading this book is that you will wisely listen to the stories and learn.

In the western highlands of Virginia, the last generation of mountain people continues to live where their ancestors have lived for hundreds of years. Although they now have the amenities of basic living, such as electricity, telephones, and indoor plumbing, these hearty Appalachian folk remember what life was like before such luxuries.

They grew up in small communities that had names such as White Rock, Tyro, Montebello, Chicken Holler, and Love. They lived in multigenerational cabins that had little in the way of modern conveniences. Each mountain hamlet was a self-contained unit that served the people living in and around its boundaries. In the late nineteenth and early twentieth centuries, many folks did not have vehicles and relied on foot power or horses to take them where they wanted to go.

I remember talking to a man who thought nothing of walking twenty miles to another community to attend a Saturday night dance held at someone's home. The family where the dance was being held would move all the interior furniture to the yard so that people would have room to move freely in the house while swirling to a Virginia reel, two-step, or some personal flat footing. Many times these dances were given by families as payback to neighbors who had stepped in to help gather crops, build a barn, or do some other type of large project. In fact, dancing aside, lending a hand to a neighbor was a given, without any monetary payment expected for services rendered. Sooner or later, the person on the receiving end would reciprocate the favor by helping someone else.

Each community had its own church, school, blacksmith shop, gristmill, and general store from which to buy necessities such as coffee, sugar, and baking powder. But these rugged, self-sufficient individuals didn't need much in the way of store-bought items; they grew and raised what was needed for everyday life in the isolated mountain regions they called home.

How I came to be living among the mountain people and preserving their early culture is something I can only believe was ordained by God. I moved to Chesterfield County, Virginia, at the end of 1969; ten years later, I made another move to the tiny mountain hamlet of Love. When people found out

Introduction

I was going to Love, they told me that the mountain people were clannish, wary, and didn't cozy up to "outsiders."

My boss at the time said, "Lynn, you've built up this fantasy about living a simple, rustic life in the Blue Ridge, and it won't nearly be as good as you've imagined it."

Six months later, I called him back and said, "You know, Bill, you were right; it isn't as good as I imagined it to be. It's even *better!*" He said right then that he knew I wouldn't be coming back to Richmond.

If you are holding this book and haven't read any of the four prior Backroads books I've written about the Appalachian culture—for you, I will say, right from the get-go, the native highland people are not anything like the stereotype hillbilly image the media makes them out to be. After moving here, I found them not only welcoming but kind, considerate, and generous to a fault. I pestered my older neighbors with endless questions: how and when do you plant gardens and dig ginseng, how do you make apple butter and pickled beets, and what, exactly, are hoecake, foxfire, and extract wood?

Looking back, it's a wonder they just didn't say, "Beat it, kid!" But they had stories to tell, and I had an eager ear to listen. They patiently took me under their wing and taught me well, fulfilling my dream of living a simple, rustic lifestyle in the Virginia mountains. Better yet, they let me interview them and take their pictures to print in the *Backroads* newspaper that I published for twenty-five years.

After that, they let me write their life stories in five books that represent the mountain people and their unique culture. They dug through cigar boxes of old photographs and entrusted me with aged black-and-white originals so that I could make copies. I handled the precious cargo with kid gloves, knowing that what I was looking at was a visual record of times past. And that time has just *about* passed and is the reason I decided to write *Mountain Folk*.

Once again, I stuck close to home, talking with the people I know best, trying to capture their early remembrances before they fade away completely. They are to be revered and thanked for their invaluable contribution to the world.

Read thoughtfully the words of those who lived in the Blue Ridge Mountains of Virginia and made quiet history that will never again be replicated.

You live as long as you are remembered.

—Russian Proverb

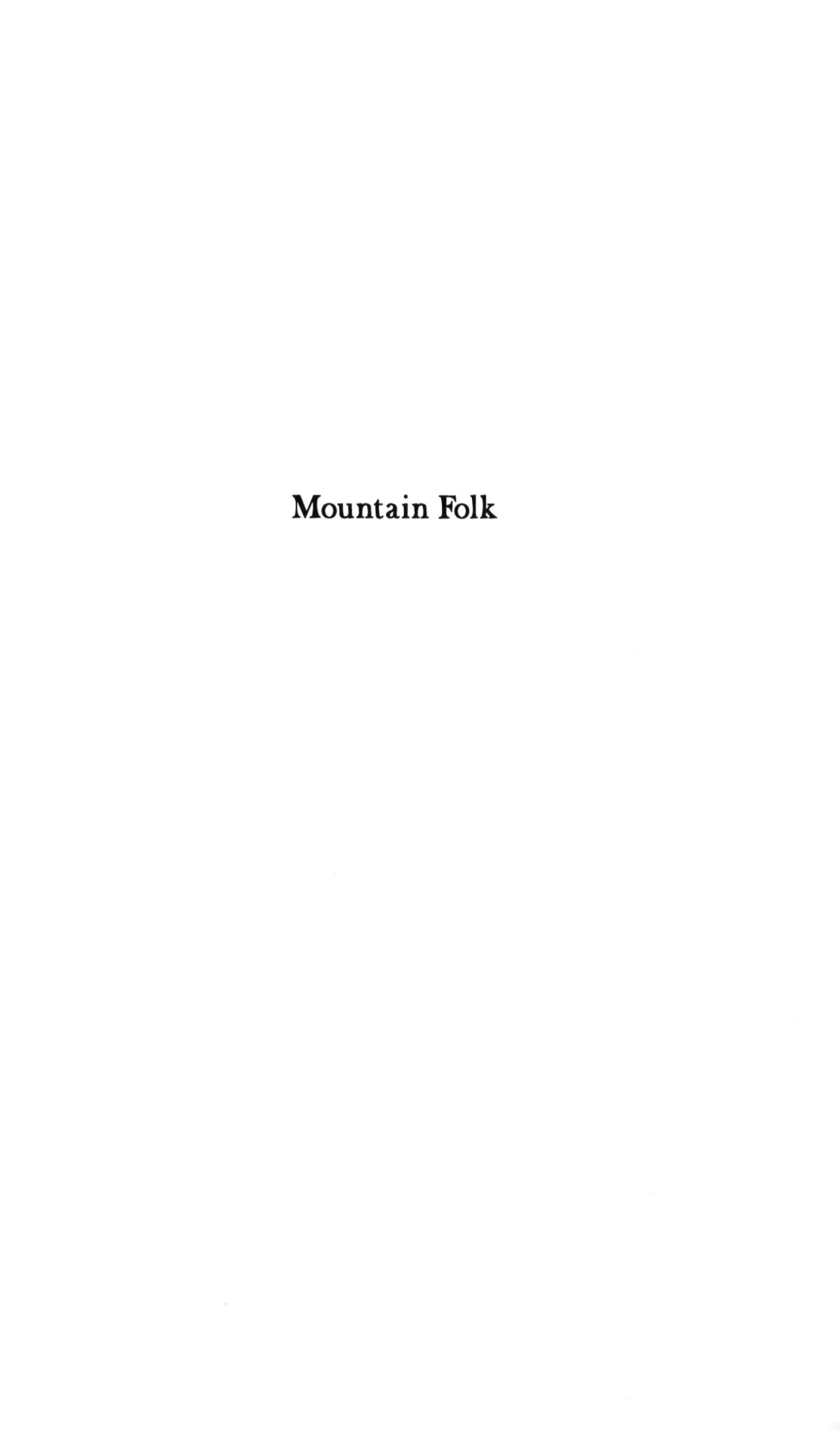

Mountain Folk

Ruby May Cook Henderson

1

Ruby May Cook Henderson

My husband, Billy, was the first to meet Ruby May after he began pastoring for Hebron Baptist Church in Afton, Virginia, in the summer of 2012. At that time, Ruby was living at the Waynesboro Manor facility in Waynesboro, Virginia. After one visit with Ruby, Billy came home and said, "You *really* need to meet this lady. She talked about growing up during horse-and-buggy days and all the things you are crazy about!"

Sure enough, he was right. Talking with Ruby transported one back to a time in history that is all but gone now. In fact, she was the inspiration for writing this fifth book about the people of Virginia's highlands. If I hadn't met Ruby May, I may never have decided to write *Mountain Folk*, and this slice of early history may have been lost. So thank you for letting me write your life story, Ruby May. At one hundred years of age, you have given the world the irreplaceable gift of your memories. Many thanks from those of us who have a heart connection to an earlier century and hold your memories dear!

I came to talk to Ruby at the end of July 2014, just a few weeks after her hundredth birthday party, which was given by Margo and Connie Miller and held at Hebron church. I came armed with a tape recorder and a million questions that I wanted to ask this plucky, soft-spoken lady. I brought her a pint of my bread-and-butter pickles. When we sat down, she served me a cup of steaming black coffee, saying, "I got to have my drinks ice cold or red hot!" At that moment I knew she was definitely a woman after my own heart.

Ruby May Cook was the last of four children born to William Henry Cook and Annie Virginia Snell Cook, who farmed and were owners of the family orchard (referred to as "the upper place") in Afton, Virginia. They raised apples and peaches on their twenty-six-acre farm that sat at the base of the Blue Ridge Mountains in a place called Fox Hollow. In the early years, Ruby said, her father, whom they called "Will," harvested the fall apples and packed them in wooden barrels. They were then hauled in a horse-drawn wagon up the mountain to the village of Afton and loaded on a train bound for various destinations.

Will bought the barrels at the cooper shop, operated by Leslie Philmore Critzer, that was located a short distance away in Avon along Goodwin Creek. In later years, Will bought

Ruby May at her hundredth birthday party

Ruby's mother: Annie Virginia Snell Cook

Ruby's father: William Henry Cook

a truck to haul his produce to the depot and to local stores that bought fruit. Ruby laughed at the memory of riding down the road in the truck while her father tried to teach her mother how to drive. "I was sitting in the back, crying!" she exclaimed.

Although there was a house on the Fox Hollow farm that the family lived in for a time, the Cooks mostly lived full time in another home on fourteen acres of land; it was closer to the main road and not far from the orchard. That home was all on one floor and had six rooms. There the family had their garden and farm animals, and it was where the Cook children were raised. Ruby May was born on Sunday, July 12, 1914. I had a good laugh as Ruby told me that when she was older, she had questioned her mother about where she came from and was told that they'd found her in a rotten stump!

Ruby's older siblings, by order of birth, were: William Henry, Jr.; Annie; and Emily. To differentiate the brother and sister who were named after their parents, William, Jr., was called "Henry," and because Ruby's mother always went by the

Top row: Henry; bottom row (from left to right) Ruby May, Emily, friend Clara Floyd, and Annie

name "Jenny," Ruby's sister was called "Annie." Henry was eight years older than Ruby, Annie was five years older, and there was a three-year difference between Ruby and Emily.

Growing up, Ruby May helped with all the work associated with farm living. She milked the cow, made butter, washed clothes, ironed, hoed the garden (unless, as Ruby says, "I could get out of it"), gathered in

The Cook siblings later in life

crops, went to the henhouse for eggs, and occasionally killed a chicken and plucked it for Sunday dinner. She did what had to be done outside but always preferred being inside, doing more domestic things like sewing, quilting, cooking, and baking.

Ruby said that her sister Emily was just the opposite; she was the tomboy of the family and loved being outside. "She could play baseball just as good as any of the boys and was always asked to play on their teams." When I asked her for more details on the individual chores she did as a child, Ruby was glad to oblige.

"Down in the fall, Mama worked in the apples, and Annie and Emily were at school, so I had to milk the cow. I guess I got tired of doing it, and one day I threw myself on the ground and told Mama, 'I ain't gonna milk Sally no more!' Mama just laughed and stepped right on by me, and I milked later on that day." Ruby May confided that many years later, after all the children were grown and gone, her mother had died while she was out milking the cow. Apparently, she had suffered a stroke and never recovered. She is buried beside her husband in the Hebron Baptist Church cemetery, where the Cook family were lifelong members.

When asked if she had ever made butter, Ruby said, "Oh yes, I've churned many a day." She used a crock-type churn with a long wooden paddle that moved up and down. Once the butter was made, it was stored in a container inside the springhouse where there was a trough that cold water ran through, keeping the butter, milk, and other perishable foods cool. These were the days before anyone had electricity, but Ruby May said that the springhouse did a good job of keeping things from spoiling.

The family had a well just outside the house where water could be pumped by hand for everything from their morning coffee to washing clothes to the proverbial Saturday night bath.

In the fall, huge threshing machines would come to cut the grain grown on the various farms. In a joint effort, neighbors helped one another get the harvest in. After the grain heads were cut, fresh straw was added to the ticks used as mattresses. Ruby said that in addition to the straw, "Mama saved all the feathers from the chickens and made feather tick mattresses and feather pillows for the beds."

I asked Ruby May if she'd ever washed clothes outside. I got a look that told me that was the dumbest question I had come up with yet! After I'd gotten done being embarrassed, I asked Ruby to describe the Monday morning ritual.

The first question she asked *me* was, "Have you ever seen a scrub board? That's what we used to get our clothes clean. We had a black pot with legs on the bottom, and we built a fire underneath it to get the water boiling. We had another tub filled with water, and we scrubbed our whites in that first. We used bar lye soap that was made from grease that was saved from butchering, and that got your clothes real clean. After we scrubbed the white clothes, they were put into the boiling water and stirred around with a stick. Then we put them in rinse water and then in bluing water."

Bluing was a liquid that acted much like today's bleach to get the clothes their whitest. The clothes were then hung on a line to dry. In the winter months, Ruby said that they did their washing in the kitchen, getting the water hot on top of the wood cookstove.

Tuesday was always ironing day, and several flatirons were kept heating on the stove for uninterrupted use. The large kitchen stove was where they did all their cooking, and Ruby thinks that it was a Home Comfort brand. It had a warming closet across the top where food could be kept warm until it was ready for the table. Food was prepared in cast-iron skillets and pots.

Ruby said that she always loved cooking, and, after her sister Annie married, all the cooking was turned over to Ruby. Her mother, who was an excellent seamstress and sewed for other people before she was married, taught her youngest daughter the craft. Ruby remembers sewing her first dress at age twelve or thirteen. "Mama went to town and brought back some pretty gingham material, and I cut it out and sewed it together and put a ruffle on it. I've been sewing ever since!" They sewed by hand and with a treadle machine that her mother had.

Ruby also learned to quilt from her mother and said, "We had a quilting frame up in the house the whole winter." Although they pieced different patterns, mostly it was just squares of material sewn together to make a colorful "crazy quilt."

I asked the names of some neighbors living around them, and Ruby laughed and said, "More Cooks!" There were also Pugh's and a family by the name of Diggs. Ruby recited a little poem that was made up about the people who lived close: "Cook's Town, Pugh Street, Diggs's Hotel, and nothing to eat!"

Hearing the little rhyme prompted me to ask if they did indeed have enough to eat. Ruby May replied, "My goodness of life, we raised all our food. We had a big garden with corn, cucumbers, beans, and tomatoes. Back then, people saved their seeds from one season to the next. We raised our chickens, we raised our pigs, and we had milk."

When asked what her mother fixed for a typical breakfast, Ruby replied, "Hot biscuits, ham and eggs or sausage and milk gravy." She said that she always loved corn bread, but her mother only seemed to make "light bread" (white bread). "Papa's brother, Uncle Ernest, and his wife lived across the road from us, and my aunt made corn bread all the time. One day, I told my mother I was going to move in with them!"

Christmas in the Cook household was a much less commercial holiday than it is now, and it focused on the birth of Jesus. There was special Christmas music at Hebron Church, and Ruby May's mother cooked a big dinner with all kinds of cakes and pies that the family enjoyed together. In the fall, all the children would get new shoes for school, and they saved the shoe boxes to line up on Christmas Eve so that Santa could leave them presents.

Ruby's Christmas tea set

Ruby's toy sewing machine

"Mostly it was a bit of candy, oranges, some nuts, and those old dried up grapes [raisins] that I never liked!" The children also received some kind of toy, and Ruby said that she always loved to play with her doll babies. One year, Santa brought a hand-painted miniature tea set, and Ruby's brother, Henry, gave her a tiny set of silverware to go along with the china; she still has it today. She also treasures a toy sewing machine that could actually stitch material together.

The Cooks worshipped at Hebron Baptist Church, and Ruby May remembers that Rev. Howard Irvine was one of the preachers there when she was a young girl. Services were held on the second and fourth Sundays because Rev. Irvine preached at other churches on the first and third ones of the month.

On the alternate Sundays, the Cook family attended Rodes United Methodist Church, located just a short distance from Hebron. "I always teased and said I was going to join the Methodist Church," Ruby said, "because their preacher could sing! We never had a preacher at Hebron who was a good singer."

People walked to church, or wherever they were going, and never thought anything about it. The back roads and the main road (Rt. 151) were gravel and didn't have as much traffic on them at that time.

When asked if they had Sunday school back then, Ruby emphatically stated, "My goodness of life, that was our main thing—going to church on Sunday! In those days, they had big meetings, and the church was crowded. In the summer, we would go to the homecoming service and revival meetings, which were held every night. Mama was an excellent seamstress and would make me a new dress, and all us children were allowed to sit up front on the bottom step where the pulpit stood on a raised platform. We thought that was really something! That was when services were held in the old sanctuary, which I loved the best. I can remember being there when they put the new stained-glass windows in."

Blue Ridge School

Ruby was a student at the Blue Ridge School, which was located next to Rodes United Methodist Church and is now a part of the church property. The school originally went up to the seventh grade, and two high school grades were added at the Rockfish School, some distance away. To go to the high school, the children had to ride a bus. Ruby May's mother didn't want her going so far from home, so Ruby quit school after the seventh grade.

In later years, Ruby said that she regretted not going "when I had more sense." One of Ruby's teachers, who taught her from third to sixth grade, was Miss Worth Dawson. She was the one who began calling Ruby May by her first and middle name, because there was another girl in the class by the name of Ruby, also. Subjects taught were geography, history, spelling, and arithmetic; the first two were Ruby May's least favorites, and arithmetic was her favorite.

When asked if they'd had spelling bees, Ruby said, "Yes, but I was no good at it!" The only time Miss Dawson, who was always so kind, ever laughed at one of her students was during a spelling bee when a pupil was asked to spell the word "buzzard." The child recited B-U-Zab-Zab-A-R-D. Ruby said, "Everyone in the class started laughing, and Miss Dawson just broke down."

Ruby said that the Afton post office was located where it stands today: right in the middle of the village, across the road from the train depot. When asked if they'd had to drive all the way up the mountain to get their mail, Ruby said, "No, in the early days, they brought the mail to the house by horse and buggy." The postmaster was Mr. Garwood, and his son, Bruce, carried the rural-route mail for years.

She also remembers that there were two stores in the Afton village, where you could buy groceries and general mercantile products: Goodloes and Dawson's. Harold Haven and his brother ran a garage where people could get their vehicles worked on. Farther down the mountain, in Glass Hollow, a man by the name of McGregor owned a mill where people could have their grain ground. "My Uncle Lewis worked there as the miller."

Neighbors had a way of entertaining themselves, and Ruby May said that the different families would have dances where young and old alike could come and have a good time. Musicians would come with their fiddles, guitars, and banjoes and play familiar tunes to which the folks would square dance, two-step, and waltz. In her own home, the Cooks had a Victrola, her brother, Henry, played the "juice harp," and the family had a peddle organ. "Henry, Annie, and Emily all took music lessons, but I was too young, so I learned how to play that organ by ear and could play most all the hymns I knew."

I asked Ruby if she went barefoot in the summertime, and she said, "Oh my goodness, yes! But we were not allowed to go barefoot until the first day of May, no matter how hot it got."

Ruby's father, Will, died when she was only six years old. Ruby explained, "Papa contracted typhoid fever a few years before, which left his heart weak, and he died in his sleep. I remember it was in the winter, and the fire had died down and the house was cold."

Her father was laid out in the parlor of the home, as was the custom. As a child, she was lifted up and told to "kiss your Papa goodbye" before he was buried, and since then she has never liked to view a deceased person at a funeral. After a brief service, he was buried in the cemetery at Hebron Baptist Church. After Will's death, Jenny kept running the orchard with help from family members, and it provided income for her and her children.

When she was old enough, Ruby May got a job in Waynesboro at the Stelhi Silk Mill, and when she was eighteen years old, she met her future husband, James Harmon Henderson.

Her sister Annie was married to Harmon's brother, Russell, and Ruby May went over to their house in Fishersville to visit Russell's ailing father. She ended up riding to Staunton with Harmon to get some medicine. Up to this point, Ruby said she had never dated anyone but found that she really liked Harmon, who was twelve years her senior.

They courted for about two years before marrying on June 23, 1934, at the church parsonage. Rev. Irvine pronounced them husband and wife just short of Ruby's twentieth birthday. Margo Miller noticed a slight discrepancy while looking at Ruby May's marriage certificate, which stated that she was twenty-one at the time she married. That was the legal age at the time. When asked if she had told a "little white lie," a smile crossed Ruby's face. She told Margo, "Before I left home that day, I wrote the number twenty-one on a piece of paper and slipped it inside my shoe. When they asked my age, I said I was 'over' twenty-one!"

When they married, Harmon was a salesman, but later he found employment at the Hamilton-Cook Hardware Store in Waynesboro. The couple's first son, Harmon Watkins "Buddy" Henderson, was born at home on December 12, 1935. Dr. Weems was supposed to come for the delivery but had another patient in labor in the hospital, so he sent his associate, Dr. Watkins, instead. Buddy was named for the man who brought him into the world.

The Henderson's second child, a daughter named Barbara Lee, was born on December 23, 1939, and their youngest son, Donald Henry, came on January 7, 1955, twenty years after Buddy was born.

Henderson family portrait

Ruby May was a housewife who enjoyed staying home to raise her children. She continued her love of sewing and baking throughout the years and even made a beautiful four-tiered wedding cake for Buddy's marriage.

When the children were older, Ruby did seamstress work at the Southern Department Store in Waynesboro and participated in the fall Apple Days Festival, winning several first-place ribbons for her beautiful sewing.

When Ruby's youngest son, Donnie, was

Buddy's wedding cake that Ruby made

just thirteen years of age, Ruby's husband, Harmon, passed away. That was in October 1968 after thirty-four years of marriage. They say that into every life a little rain must fall, but some people seem to have more than their share of sadness. At one hundred years of age, Ruby May is the last surviving member of her family, outliving all of her siblings, her beloved husband, and her three children. Barbara passed away first in 1996, Buddy in 2007, and Donnie in 2011 with no grandchildren to carry on the Cook name. But even with such heartbreak, Ruby May has kept a positive outlook and wry humor that inspire everyone who knows her.

She has lived in various places over the years, but in March 2014, she was invited by Bill and Margo Miller to move back to Afton to a little home located on their property. This arrangement has suited everyone, especially Ruby May, who continues to enjoy handwork, blessing others with colorful knitted lap robes and the coveted knit dish rags that seem to

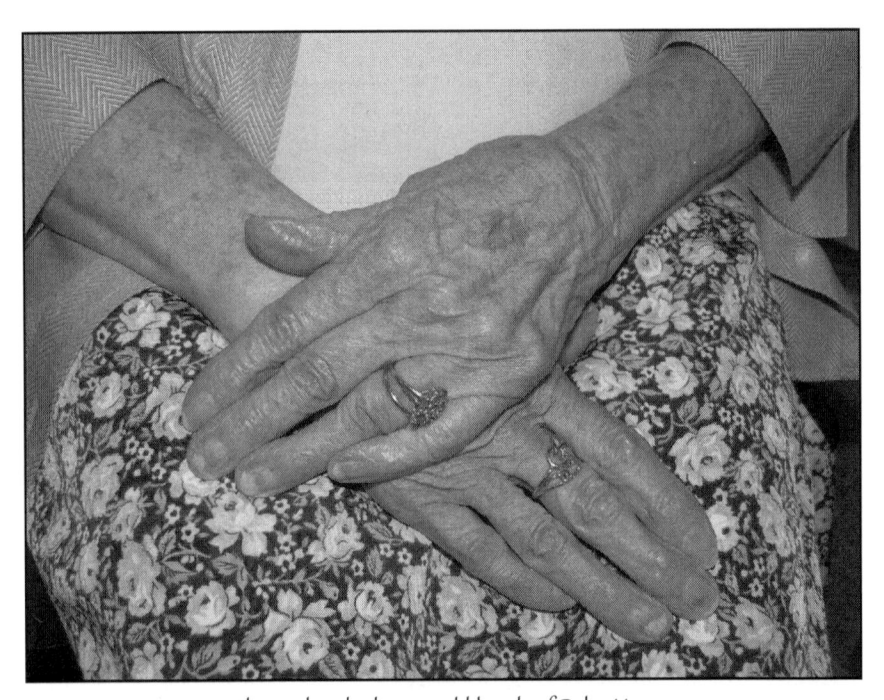

The one hundred-year-old hands of Ruby May

last forever. In fact, after the interview, she surprised me with a lovely pale lavender lap robe on which she was just putting the finishing touches.

So Ruby May Henderson's life has come full circle, back to where she started and happy to spend time with her extended family as well as any friends who come to visit.

May God bless you richly, Ruby, for all your years of faithfulness to God and others.

Ronald Massie "Butch" Taylor

2

Ronald Massie "Butch" Taylor

Butch Taylor and his family have always been part of my life here on the mountain. I remember driving over to their homeplace in White Rock, the Friday night before trout fishing season began, to listen to music and talk with the folks who came out for the annual celebration along the North Fork of the Tye. Billy and I will never forget the mountain supper William Henry Coffey and Don Taylor cooked for us: fried cabbage, brown beans, tenderloin, and crisp cornbread, just the way Billy likes it. In fact, he made me get William Henry's recipe that night so I could make the cornbread of Billy's youth.

Butch's wife, Mary Lee, suggested we meet for the interview at their homeplace. The road to White Rock is one of my favorites; a narrow gravel lane that winds deep in the mountains and passes familiar landmarks, such as Evergreen Christian Church, the old Alec Coffey homeplace, the Massie Camp, White Rock Cemetery, Miz Nettie Taylor's log cabin, and a wealth of other places where the people I've talked to over the years have lived.

It was an unusually crisp August morning when I made the trip down Campbell's Mountain Road, up Route 56, then onto Route 687 to White Rock. I always remember the route number because Preacher Billy Morris, who lived on the road, told me, "Route 687 . . . closest thing to heaven!" Another amazing thing about the twenty-mile round trip over to White Rock that morning was that I never passed one car on the way over or on my way back. That's why I love the back roads!

The old White Rock schoolhouse today

The coffee was on when I stepped into the old White Rock schoolhouse that Butch and Mary Lee now own and use as a camp, and picture albums were waiting on the table. Some of the family photos dated back to 1902, and I recognized many of the people in the pictures from years before when I did articles about them in *Backroads* newspaper. It struck me as funny that people I had never known and who had died fifty years before I ever came here were so recognizable to me.

Members of the Taylor, Coffey, and Fitzgerald families mostly made their homes in this little tucked-away mountain village, and history has left its indelible mark. Butch pointed out many initials carved into the back wall of the schoolhouse, probably etched with a knife by young boys who had been sent out to stand alone as punishment. All the initials ended with either a T, C, or an F. One clearly stood out: O. W. T., which stood for Orcie Wilmer Taylor, Butch's dad.

I teased Butch about finally getting around to interviewing him personally, because in years past, he was "too young" to be one of those about whom I traditionally wrote articles. *Backroads* newspaper covered three generations of mountain people: the grandparents, parents, and, now, the children who had grown up in the Blue Ridge. So Butch, at sixty-eight years of age—you qualify! Thanks for all these years of friendship.

━━━⁂━━━

Ronald Massie "Butch" Taylor, born on June 15, 1946, was the third and youngest son of Orcie Wilmer Taylor and Gladys Green Coffey Taylor. Older brothers Sonny and Don were born in 1942 and 1944, respectively. All three, I was surprised to learn, were born at the Lynchburg Hospital, instead of at home with a midwife.

When Gladys was ready to deliver her firstborn, a midwife was with her, and Doctor Kennan, who had a practice in Raphine, was supposed to come to the house to deliver the baby, but when they called him, he wouldn't come. The midwife told Orcie to take his wife to the Lynchburg Hospital, because she couldn't seem to help her. When Sonny was finally born on July 4, 1942, he weighed more than ten pounds.

Sonny's given name was Safard Cliel, named by Margie Coffey Hatter, who grew up across the river. Don Wilmer came next, on October 25, 1944, weighing in at only four pounds—quite a difference from his brother—to the relief of his mother!

Butch's grandparents on his father's side were Henry and Zimena Taylor. Maternal grandparents were Charlie and Teressie Coffey. Both sets of grandparents lived in and around the White Rock area. Zimena, whom they called "Ziney," died of tuberculosis in her twenties.

The homeplace where the Taylors lived stands on property along the Tye River just below the old schoolhouse that Butch now owns. Although he doesn't know how old the structure is, he said that his grandfather Henry had once lived there, and Hercy Coffey, who owned the mill across the river from the Taylors, once had a store in the building before later building one next to his mill.

Butch said that Randolph Hite would walk down the mountain from where he lived at the end of Chicken Holler, go to Hercy's store, then come back via Butch's house and give him a candy bar.

Lura Coffey Steele, whose parents were Hercy and Burgess Coffey, said that her family was living in the Taylor home when she was born there on December 24, 1922. In 1923, her daddy made one of the rooms into the little store that Butch was talking about. She also remembers her daddy and Jim Taylor running a saw mill that was set in a little flat in front of the house. Years later, Butch's brother Don and Don's wife, Sue, bought the homeplace from their parents, and it is still in that family.

The Taylor homeplace at White Rock

Orcie, Gladys, and their three sons lived in the home until Butch was six years old. Butch remembers that his Grandma Teressie, who at that time had moved down from the hollow along Spring Branch and was living in the schoolhouse, would watch him and his brothers while his parents drove to Stuarts Draft to work at the Rockingham chicken processing plant.

The Taylors' pay at that time was fifty cents an hour, so they brought home twenty dollars a week apiece. Because of the traveling distance, the decision was made to move closer to the job, so the family moved to Stuarts Draft in November 1952.

Orcie bought a farmhouse on two acres from a man by the name of Wade Cline, and Orcie and Gladys lived there for the rest of their lives. Butch said that the old house had two big rooms downstairs and two rooms upstairs, and although it was hooked up with electricity, they still didn't have any indoor plumbing. There was a cistern under the house where rainwater was caught and stored until pumped by hand into buckets that were then brought into the house.

In 1943, while they were still living on the North Fork, Orcie Taylor was drafted into the navy and served two years; he came home to White Rock in 1945.

I asked Butch if he remembered living at the homeplace, and he said that although he

Butch's parents, Orcie and Gladys Taylor (1945)

was young at the time, he could remember that Sonny had a dog to which they attached a harness to help pull stove wood out of the woods. Later on, that job fell to Butch himself, while his older brothers had bigger responsibilities.

Gladys had a wood cookstove. Butch said that one time, Sonny decided to fix some eggs and about blew the whole house up. "Sonny put gasoline on the fire, thinking it was kerosene, and it exploded with all these flames boiling up. We were by ourselves, and he couldn't have been more than eight or nine years old at the time. Another time, Don and I were playing, and we wrapped Sonny up in some kind of an old coat on the porch, and we just about had him smothered when our parents came in."

Butch can also remember that when he was around five, he complained about having a bad stomach ache; Doctor Dickie examined him and found he had appendicitis. He was sent to the hospital in Charlottesville to have his appendix removed. On another occasion, he had a stay in the old Waynesboro Hospital (now McDow Funeral Home) to have his tonsils taken out.

(Top row) cousin Ruthie Fitzgerald and Sonny; (bottom row) Don and Butch (1951)

Butch attended the White Rock Christian Church, which was located up the hill from the schoolhouse, but not on a regular Sunday basis, because the preacher split his time between other congregations. They held yearly homecoming services to which came many people who had ties in the area.

Once again, when talking with Lura Steele, she reported that the church was "new" in 1890 and had been established by H. Davis Coffey. He was responsible for many of the early Christian churches around the mountainous areas of Nelson County, including Mountain Top at Love, Wintergreen at Wintergreen, and Evergreen on the North Fork near Nash, all of which continue to hold Sunday services.

Early preachers at all the churches were: Davis Coffey; Riley Fitzgerald; Revs. Crist, Boyd, and Leake; and Bob Allen. The last service held in the church was Martin Fitzgerald's funeral in April 1960, and Bob Allen was the preacher.

The Taylors hooked up to the electric line that came through White Rock around 1950, and Butch's daddy bought a radio from Sears that was delivered by mail. Everyone from all over came to the house on Saturday nights to listen to the Grand Ole Opry. "I remember people sittin' around the walls, everywhere."

White Rock Church with school at left (1930s)

The White Rock congregation (1942)

Speaking of the mail delivery, Butch said that more than once, Mr. Roscoe Floyd, the rural route carrier at that time, threatened to throw Butch's tricycle into the river if he didn't quit leaving it in the road! Butch actually beat him to it when he rode off a hill and got up so much speed he couldn't stop and ended up in White Rock Creek.

Roscoe Floyd, mail carrier in the 1950s

I asked where the nickname "Butch" came from, and he said that he didn't know, but offered, "I must have gotten into a lot of stuff. Most Butches did! We came back over here one time after we had moved for a picnic Uncle Otis was having, and I sneaked off and walked up to Wallace's [Wallace Oliver] Flat, which is above Durham's Run. Tommy Taylor saw me and picked me up in his Model A and brought me back to the homeplace where everyone was looking for me."

The current White Rock school building was thought to have been constructed by Jake Allen in 1910. Before that time, Butch's grandma, Teressie

Burgess Coffey in front of the White Rock school (1940)

Coffey, had said that there used to be a one-room log schoolhouse behind where the new school was built. Venie Fitzgerald, born in 1902, said that they held school inside the White Rock Church before the new school was finished. The school at White Rock closed at the end of the school term in 1947, so Butch started school at Fleetwood Elementary in Massies Mill.

Butch at eight years of age

Halfway through the year, the family moved to Stuarts Draft, and he attended first grade in the old brick two-story Stuarts Draft School on Main Street. For some of the earlier grades, the children were switched over to the new school across the road, but they went back to the old building to finish the seventh grade in Miss Crummet's class.

Butch started high school at Wilson Memorial in Fishersville but decided to end his formal education when he was about sixteen years old in favor of going to work. He added, "That's when my life started." It was 1962, the same time he met his future wife, Mary Lee Buchanan, at the Raphine carnival.

Mary Lee was the daughter of Henry Buchanan and Clara Mae Potter Buchanan of Spottswood, and she had just graduated from Spottswood High School. The next year, Mary Lee went to Wilson High School, three hours a day for nine months, to begin training for a career in nursing. She finished up at King's Daughters Hospital in Staunton, where she got her LPN degree. She made a career of nursing, working at King's Daughters, the Waynesboro hospital, and the new Augusta Health Hospital, which combined the two other hospitals in 1994. Mary Lee retired in May 1997 because of ongoing health issues.

Butch started out working for a company based in Lynchburg that was laying telephone lines; later he worked as a mechanic's helper at Cliff's Garage in Stuarts Draft. That was when Main Street, Stuarts Draft, was booming. Some of the other stores at that time were: Engleman's Hardware, Hockman's Grocery, a bank, a drug store, the Variety Store, and Cohron's Hardware as well as a few other businesses.

Butch was working at Blue Ridge Grocery in Waynesboro when he and Mary Lee got married on December 5, 1964. Guy Stump, pastor at Mount Vernon Church of the Brethren, married the couple in his home; then the pair lived with Mary Lee's mother for a time before buying a four-room home on Wilda Road from Dennis and Vivian Allen. The Taylors added onto the home over the years, and they continue to reside there.

After the wedding, Butch went to work for Roy Harner Excavating in Waynesboro. He drove a dump truck and later learned to run heavy equipment. He worked there for two years. A man by the name of Roy Harris had a woodyard at the railroad up on Cold Spring, and he needed someone to run a knuckle boom, so Butch left Harner to begin work there. In the meantime, he bought a ton truck, and after a full day at the woodyard, he would go out and cut a load of pulpwood with Dale Allen.

Butch worked with Dale for ten years in the logging business; at times, Butch's brothers, Sonny and Don, helped out, too. Others Butch worked with over the years were: Ever-

Butch and Mary Lee's wedding picture

A full load of logs ready for the lumberyard

ett Allen, William Henry Coffey, Dennis and Butch Allen, Manley Allen, and Ronnie Allen. Butch said, "Ronnie's dad, Dennis, would bid on Forest Service boundaries within the National Forest in Big Levels Game Preserve on the Coal Road, and we would cut pine off those tracts."

Butch and Mary Lee's first child, Jesse Wayne, was born on September 13, 1968; Nancy Ann came on August 24, 1971. Billy Coffey married Jesse to Rebecca "Becky" Noel Swisher on November 20, 2010, at Evergreen Christian Church. Jesse and Becky live next to his parents with Becky's two children from a previous marriage, Cody and Taylor Ann Swisher. Nancy married Greg Varner and moved to Mount Solon. The Varners have two daughters, Taylor Ann (17) and Hannah Marie (14).

Butch quit logging with Dale to try other ventures, and it was at this time that Mitch Carr, a Montebello-born man who had established the Augusta Lumber mills, asked Butch to come to work for him. Butch said that he worked at the Staunton mill for a time, then made a move to the mill in North Garden. Mitch's brother, Howard, was the general manager there.

A Taylor family portrait

Butch ran a loader and unloaded the log trucks. He did this for about two years, then he started buying logs from the local loggers as they came to the mill. Later, he helped get veneer logs ready for export. After that, he became the mill manager and continued to run the log yard. Augusta Lumber was one of the biggest exporters of logs and lumber in the state at the time.

Andy Moore came to work with Butch; eventually, he took over the log yard, and Butch just helped out at times. The mill became so large that another man, by the name of Earl Thompson, had to be hired. The mill operated from 7:00 a.m. until 7:00 p.m. five days a week with a half day on Saturdays. When dealing with veneer logs in the winter, the men would sometimes work seven days week, twenty-four hours a day to keep the saw mill operating around the clock.

Butch is quick to add, "I could not have worked like this had it not been for a good wife at home. Mary Lee was working at the hospital eight- and twelve-hour shifts, plus taking care of the children and everything else at home."

White oak veneer logs

Stacks of four-by-four lumber

Bear-hunting party at Eddie Allen's place (2005)

Eventually Augusta Lumber was sold, and Butch left after thirty years of service. He said, "I enjoyed working for and with Mitch and Howard Carr. They were like family to me and let me take off work for hunting season."

Butch Taylor, like most of the men raised up in the mountains, is a longtime hunter. Some deer and squirrels but mostly bear hunting, which is still a very popular sport here in the Blue Ridge. He's hunted with a lot of the Allens and said that one of the biggest bears taken was the one killed by Jackie Lowery that was featured in *Backroads* newspaper. The bear weighed in at 550 pounds, which is a *big* bear!

The Taylors still enjoy camping and spending time along the North Fork at the old schoolhouse with their family. They celebrated their fiftieth anniversary milestone in December 2014.

After we wound up the interview, and all the pictures had been taken, I headed back up the mountain toward home. A few days later, I had to call Mary Lee back for more information, because while listening to the recording, I discovered the machine had "eaten" the tape toward the end. I told her that

Butch and Mary Lee at their homeplace

Billy had suggested that I upgrade my technology to a digital recorder. Anyone who knows me already understands what an unwilling student I am with any type of electronics having more than an "on-and-off" button.

Mary Lee agreed, then proceeded to say the funniest and truest statement I've ever heard for anyone over sixty: "You almost have to have a kid with you!"

Audrey Carol Campbell Smegal

3

Audrey Carol Campbell Smegal

I formally met Carol and her husband, Fred, back in the early 2000s when they attended Cornerstone Baptist Church in Tyro, Virginia, where Billy pastored. But I'm sure we must have bumped heads at some of the Campbell family reunions before that. The Campbells are one of the original families who settled in this area, and Carol's particular branch of the family tree lived along Campbell Creek, near the bottom of Campbell's Mountain Road. Just by the names, you can see how many of the same family were here early on.

Carol has a vast knowledge of genealogy and was able to share a lot of information concerning her own family history. She also supplied one of the rare early photos of the Campbell Creek School and the children who were attending there at the time. I have been looking for a photo of the school for many, many years, and people who were born and raised here also said that they would give anything to have a photograph of it. For that reason alone, Carol made a lot of people very happy when she decided to be interviewed for *Mountain Folk*. Thank you, Carol, for your invaluable contribution!

Although Carol left the mountains when an older teenager to find work, as a child she was raised up the old way. In 1991, she returned with her husband and grandson to the same area in Nelson County, Virginia, that she'd originally called home.

Her parents were Richard Raymond "Red" Campbell, who was born in 1908, and Olettia Little Heart Fitzgerald Campbell, born in 1910. The Campbells were married on December 21, 1931, in Lovingston, Virginia, after Olettia turned twenty-one in September of the same year.

Family tales that had been passed down told the story of how Carol's mother got her unusual name. One of Olettia's uncles began fighting in the Civil War as a Confederate but later deserted and went over to the Union side. The northern army didn't trust him, so they sent him out west to fight the Indians. Carol stated, "Mama always said one of her uncles named her," and Carol feels that while he was out west, the Indian culture must have influenced the name he insisted on calling his niece.

Olettia's parents were Perry Dickerson Fitzgerald and Rosa Lee Coffey Fitzgerald.

Carol's parents, Richard and Olettia Campbell

They had six children and lived in the same general area of Nelson County as the Campbell side of the family.

Richard Campbell's parents were Oscar Parker Campbell and Dora Elphalay Fitzgerald Campbell, and they had seven children.

The Campbell family originally settled in the mountainous area of Campbell's Creek, and records show that one of Oscar's brothers, Francis Jefferson Campbell, bought 386 acres in December 1794, although there were other members of the same family who owned land up the same hollow. Carol said that her great-uncle's house was always referred to as the "Jeff House" when she was growing up. The Coffey and Fitzgerald families also owned land around the same location, and all three families are interrelated.

Carol's grandfather Oscar lived on a piece of land that was part of his father's large tract. The original cabin located there had burned down in the 1920s, so Oscar built a new one.

Carol's maternal grandparents, Perry and Rosa Lee Fitzgerald, with Kenneth and Watson Coffey

He lived there almost until he died in 1963; for the last few years of his life, he alternated living with his two daughters. Because Carol's immediate family later moved just down the field from Oscar's place, I asked if she remembered going to visit her grandfather and what his old cabin looked like.

She replied, "You walked in the front door,

Carol's paternal grandfather, Oscar Parker Campbell (1961)

and an old-time fireplace was on the left. In one corner of the room, a long table sat against the wall, with Granddaddy's reading material and an oil lamp set on top of it. His rocking chair was next to the table. There was an add-on kitchen to the rear of the cabin, and a bed sat on the other side of the main room, with steps going up into the attic.

"There was also an old cabin up on the mountain across the road from Granddaddy's that Mama took us on a hike to when we were small. I found an old brooch on the property, which I still have."

Carol said that she always thought the Campbells were strictly from a Scottish/Irish descent, but in going

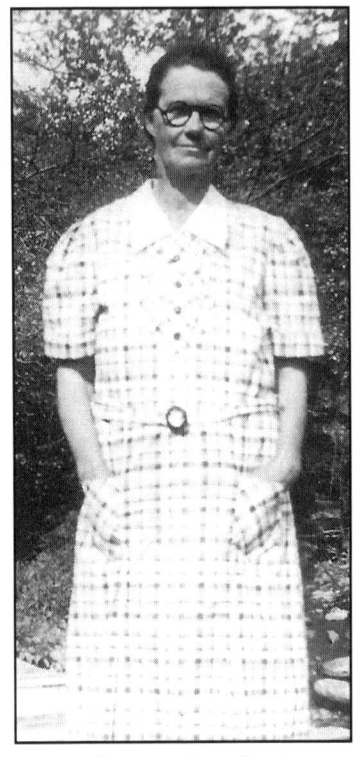

Carol's paternal grandmother, Dora Elphalay Fitzgerald Campbell

Oscar Campbell's log cabin in 1959, ten years before the '69 flood

The cabin after the flood, with rocks strewn over the property

back through early genealogy records, she found people who were of French, German, and English lineage as well. These records go back to the eleventh century, to the year 1006, when a man by the name of Duina Macduibhn was born in Scotland. In 1020, Duina had a son they named Malcome Macduibhn Campbell, and from that time on, the family last name was changed to Campbell. Duina Macduibhn died in 1066 and is buried in Normandy, France. Carol says, "So I guess we are kind of a soup-pot mixture."

After marriage, Carol's father, Richard, became a tenant farmer at Tom Carter's farm on East Branch Road in Roseland, and he and his wife lived in a small home that Mr. Carter supplied. That is where the first three of the six children were born: Marion Rudolph "Buck" on August 15, 1934; James Lewis in November 1936; and Audrey Carol on December 21, 1939, which was her parents' eighth wedding anniversary. The fourth child, Don Elliott, was born in January 1942 in a cabin they were living in after the family had moved to Tyro.

During the winter of that same year, the army came in to train men, because the conditions in the Virginia mountains were similar to Germany. "The men were marching on the road, and it was so cold that one man's feet were frozen. They came to the house, and Mama ran warm water in a tub to let him put his feet in to thaw out."

When Earl Raymond was born in March 1945, the family had moved to a house in Tyro on Battery Hill, and he was the only Campbell sibling to be born in a hospital. Carol said that the midwife who delivered most of the area's babies was Leasy Snead Adams. When the last Campbell child, Linda Gale, was born in May 1947, Richard and the kids' Aunt Nannie were there for the birth. When Linda, whom they nicknamed "Sis," was born, she was not breathing, and her dad resuscitated her; this fueled Richard's desire to become an active member of the Roseland Rescue Squad in later years.

The Campbell homeplace after the flood, where Earl still lives

The family moved around and rented from other people until Richard bought land down from his father's cabin and built a two-room house. Carol laughs at the memory. "Six of us kids in one bedroom! What would social services have to say about that today?" As time went on, the house was enlarged to accommodate the family.

Richard found work at the American Cyanamid plant in Piney River in the early 1940s and was employed there until the plant closed in 1971, leaving countless men without jobs.

The Campbells attended Evergreen Christian Church, and Carol remembers, "There was a nice grove of trees on one side of the church, and during homecoming Sunday, they put up long tables between the trees, and they would be loaded with food!" She was baptized in a deep hole of water at the forks of the Tye River down from the church. "I think that's where I got my fear of water. When Preacher Leake was baptizing me and had me under the water, his hand slipped, and he almost lost me. It scared me, and I never did learn to swim."

When Carol was a child, her mother would take them up a hill by the house to pick blackberries that were then canned for the winter. It was a time when Campbell's Mountain Road was unpaved, and people knew everyone who traveled up and down the narrow, winding road.

The family got their water from a spring located just up from the house, and that's where her mother had a spring box to keep perishable foods cool. Carol remembers that before the flood of '69, wild roses grew up the trees by the spring, making a cool, shady glen to which the children loved to go. When asked if they had indoor plumbing, Carol laughed. "No, we had *outdoor* plumbing!"

They did not get electricity until the mid-1950s, and Carol said, "Once we got electric, Daddy just had to go get a television—one of those that had the big metal cases. And I remember

Olettia Little Heart Campbell with her six children

on Saturday nights, there was always wrestling, and Berkley and Gladys Oliver would come over to watch the TV with their two daughters. One night, one of the wrestlers got knocked out of the ring, and Berkley jumps up and runs over to the TV, looking down into it to see if he could see the guy down on the floor."

Two of the Campbell siblings were hearing impaired. Buck was born a deaf-mute, and Earl was partially deaf. "Mama and Daddy began to suspect there was a problem when the boys didn't begin talking when most children their age did. I guess that gene can be passed down through the family. Granddaddy Oscar had a brother, Jimmy, who was a deaf-mute, and he went to VSDB [Virginia School for the Deaf and Blind] in Staunton, Virginia. Jimmy lived with Granddaddy in his cabin until [Jimmy] died."

They thought that Carol might have also been mute, because it took her so long to talk. She laughs and says, "Maybe I just didn't have anything to say!" When asked how they communicated with the boys, Carol said they'd made up their own sign language.

Buck didn't go to elementary school, because at that time there were no teachers equipped to handle a child with disabilities. A distant Snead relative moved back to the area when Buck was fourteen and made an application for him at VSDB. Buck was accepted and stayed at the school until he was twenty-one. When Buck started VSDB, he learned American sign language, and many of the signs were the same as what the family had already been using to communicate.

Earl started public school at Fleetwood in Massies Mill, where all the other children attended, but once again, there were no teachers trained for special-needs children, so he was also enrolled at VSDB. While at the school, both boys took upholstery and cabinet making classes so that they would have a vocation when they had to make their way in the working world. Buck's first job was at an upholstery shop in Lynchburg.

Earl graduated with honors and was accepted at a well-known college for the deaf in Washington, DC, but he knew his parents could not afford it. Also, Earl felt that he could not work full time and keep up with his studies, so he came home and found work at Stanley Furniture Company in Waynesboro. Because of their brothers' hearing impairments, both

Carol and Linda Gale taught their children and grandchildren sign language at an early age so that they could communicate with their uncles.

Carol remembers that the old Campbell Creek School had two rooms with a beadboard interior. The photo below shows a class of early students. The school faced sideways next to Campbell Creek on the Oliver property along Campbell's Mountain Road. By the time Carol was the age to start school, Campbell Creek had closed and was being used as a private residence by Berkley Oliver and his family. During the flood of 1969, the building was damaged and much of the ground it stood on was washed away, so it had to be taken down.

Early photo of the Campbell Creek School

Carol began attending Fleetwood, which had eleven grades. She remembers that two of her early bus drivers were Billy Byers from Montebello and Parrish Strickland of Tyro. At that time, Campbell's Mountain Road was just a dirt path, and the last stop was at her Uncle Clarence's house, where her cousins were picked up. Carol went through eighth grade at Fleetwood; after that, the children were bused to the new Nelson County

High School near Lovingston. The last class graduated from Fleetwood in 1955.

Carol graduated from Nelson High School in 1958 and began looking for work. Her mother would not let her move to Lynchburg to live with an aunt where she would have had a better chance of finding employment. In fact, Carol said that her mother was very protective of all her children when they were young. They were not even allowed to walk down the road to Hatter's Store, much less another store farther down the mountain that Elmer Hatter ran.

"Mama was overcautious and wanted to know where we were and what we were doing! But I remember walking home at dusk up Campbell's Creek with Aunt Margaret, and we heard a wild panther scream on the mountain. She looked at me and I looked at her, and we moved a little faster and got home!"

Carol was nineteen years old and still not having any luck finding a job. She remembers, "My brother James, who joined the navy, . . . was stationed in New Jersey when he met and married Pat Story [in 1959]. They came down to Virginia Beach on their honeymoon and stopped to visit family. When they were ready to go back to Moorestown, New Jersey, I went with them, living with Pat and her parents, because James was still in the navy.

"I decided to give myself until October to find a job, or I was going back home. Pat's mother worked in the A&P and came home and said there was a rumor they would be needing some-

Four generations of Campbells: Oscar, Richard, James, and Jimmy

one at Metropolitan Life Insurance Company to work in the office, answering phones, taking payments, and doing bookwork. This was my first experience with riding public buses, and I didn't know what to think!"

Carol met her future husband, Fred Smegal, through friends. Fred's mother had died of tuberculosis when he was six or seven, and even though Carol was three years older in age, Fred was, in Carol's words, "already an old soul." They dated for two years, marrying on June 17, 1961. Carol laughs at the memory, "Fred graduated from high school on a Wednesday, and we got married that Saturday."

The couple started out living in a succession of three small apartments in Moorestown before they saved the nine hundred dollars needed for a down payment on their first house, a small cottage. They lived there for fifteen years before buying a larger house in 1981. Fred was a typesetter at his uncle's rubber stamp business; the same job he'd held in high school before he graduated. Fred and Carol's first son, Frederick Smegal, was born on June 30, 1962, and was promptly nicknamed "Ricky" to keep confusion to a minimum, since Carol's husband was Fredrick, as was Fred's father. Their daughter, Audrey Cheryl, was born December 13, 1967. Because of family circumstances in later years, the Smegals also raised Ricky's son, Frederick Michael, whom they called "Buddy," and he continues to live with Carol.

The Smegals' wedding day; Carol's parents at left (June 17, 1961)

The Smegals were still living in New Jersey in 1969 when Hurricane Camille came through on the evening of August 19, causing untold damage. Carol said she had not heard anything about it, because back home, everyone's electricity and telephone lines were down, and there was no communication. She happened to be looking at a New Jersey newspaper when she read about what was happening in Nelson County. She had some very tense hours until she found out that the family was safe, but they had a harrowing tale to tell.

Carol's Campbell grandparents, Oscar and Dora, were already deceased, so their old cabin was empty. The upper bridge on Campbell's Mountain Road above the cabin had been ravaged by the huge amount of debris washing down the creek, and the water was being diverted down through the field and surrounding the home where Carol's parents and her brothers, Buck and Earl, were still living. The water was rising at an alarming rate, so the Campbells decided to wade with their two dogs to Oscar's cabin, which was on little higher ground.

Their cousin Dixie Lee Fitzgerald and her husband, Lester, lived across the road, and they were trapped on the opposite side of the creek. Lester was a logger, so he got his chain saw and cut a big tree down across the creek and both crawled over to the main road. Another cousin, Filmore Fitzgerald, had a house that sat higher up on the mountain, so the couple made their way up to it.

Filmore Fitzgerald's house on Campbell's Mountain Road

Once they arrived, everyone realized that Carol's family might be trapped as well, so they walked down and began yelling to them. Filmore was also a logger; he and Lester began cutting trees down over the steep bank by Oscar's cabin, and one by one Carol's family began crawling up to the safety of Filmore's house where they all waited out the terrible storm.

I asked if any lives had been lost on Campbell's Mountain Road, and Carol said no, but several houses were either washed away or damaged so badly that they had to be taken down. "Frank Campbell had a two-story house that was destroyed, and when the flood was over, the Mennonites came to help and built Cousin Frank another small house across the road on land that now belongs to Buddy and Bobbie Newton. Later, my brother Buck lived in a house that was built where Frank's original house stood. The flood also took Hatter's Store, which was on the opposite side of the road from where it is now."

Fred and Carol after they'd moved back to Virginia

Just a few short miles down the road on Route 56, things were very different. By the time Campbell's Creek converged with the Tye River, the flood waters had risen so high and gathered so much floating debris along with the mud and boulders coming down from the mountains that many homes and lives were lost.

In New Jersey, Carol's life was changing. Fred's uncle sold his rubber stamp business to a larger company that combined three similar businesses. Fred and Carol both worked for the consolidated company for years before finding new employment with a man who had started up a chain of luxury motels. The Smegals worked as night managers in the Jersey motel, and when the man built another in Philadelphia, they moved there. After working four twelve-hour shifts a week for a while, Carol said that it just got to be too much for them.

In August 1989, they decided to move to Waynesboro, Tennessee, where the Smegals, along with Fred's brother, went into the restaurant/motel business for themselves. They were doing well and had come back to Nelson County for Carol's mother's funeral in May 1991, when they received a call saying that there had been a flood; a bridge on the interstate was damaged, and traffic was being diverted around the motel.

The Smegals tried to make it through the summer with just the locals eating at the restaurant, but it wasn't enough to save them. They moved back to Virginia in October 1991, and stayed with Carol's dad and Earl until they bought a home in Lowesville. They moved into their new home in March 1993, during one of the worst blizzards the area had seen for years. Carol's father passed away in August of the same year.

Fred began looking for work and filled out an application at Con-Agra Company in Crozet. He applied for a position as a cook, but when he was interviewed and they saw his previous experience, he was hired as a manager of ASC, who ran the plant cafeteria. After a few years, the company moved Fred to Lynchburg where their offices were located. He was put in charge of the various ASC cafeterias in Virginia, West Virginia, South Carolina, and Maryland, making sure each facility was clean and procedures were being followed.

Carol soon grew bored of staying at home alone after Buddy went to school, so she got a housekeeping job at the Village Inn Motel in Lovingston and worked there until 2000 when her allergies became so bad that she had to retire from that

Oscar Campbell's log cabin (spring 2014)

position. The same year, she found new employment as a substitute teacher in the Nelson County School system.

Everything was going well until they received a late-night call early in February 2001. Their son, Ricky, had contracted bacterial pneumonia and was in the hospital ICU in New Jersey. Carol made the trip up north and stayed for three weeks until Ricky passed away on February 22, 2001. Arrangements were made, and he was brought back to Virginia to be buried at Jonesboro Baptist Church Cemetery in Roseland, where most of Carol's family is interred.

Fred was laid off from his job at ASC in 2005, so Carol stayed on teaching until spring 2006, when Fred was able to get disability because of health reasons. Fred passed away on February 18, 2007, just four days short of six years after Ricky had been laid to rest. The Smegals had been married for forty-six years at the time of his death.

Four of the six Campbell siblings still survive; Carol and her grandson "Buddy" continue to live in Lowesville. Her brother Earl lives in the homeplace on one of three small parcels of land left from Francis Campbell's original 386 acres, and he is the last remaining member of the family still living on Campbell's Mountain Road. Don lives in New Jersey, and "Sis" is in Texas.

Since childhood, Carol has always enjoyed reading. She said that her first-grade teacher, a single woman by the name

Carol and her brother Earl

of Miss Powell, instilled a love of reading in her, and she continues to be a big reader today. She and her sister are also big into family genealogy, and each October, Carol can be found at the large Campbell family reunion. In addition to her two children, Carol also has two grandchildren and four great-grandchildren.

Carol concluded our interview by saying, "We had fun growing up. We made our own fun. When they built the movie theater in Lovingston, sometimes Daddy would take all of us to a Friday night movie. That was a big deal, taking six kids to a movie! I remember the night of the '69 flood, the movie *The Longest Day* was playing. After that night, the theater closed down because of damage from the water."

What a wonderful trip down memory lane from a girl who traveled to many of the east coast states before returning to the mountains that she calls home.

Kenneth Ray Fitzgerald

4

Kenneth Ray Fitzgerald

I'm not exactly sure when I first met Kenneth. It was probably on one of my many trips to Montebello to cover a story for *Backroads* newspaper. He seemed to be everywhere at once, helping barbeque chicken for the Montebello Fire Department, stirring apple butter, cutting firewood, or herding cattle to their summer grazing grounds. If God gives everyone on earth a gift, Kenneth Fitzgerald was blessed with the gift of "helps."

Soft spoken, easy-going, and with an ever present smile, Kenneth makes everyone around him feel comfortable. When my husband became the pastor of the Mount Paran Baptist Church in 1999, we came to know Kenneth more intimately. We found he has a deep faith, and, as a Christian, he lives what he believes, making his testimony less about words and more about action. As Billy likes to say, "Tell people about God; speak if you must."

Although Kenneth is serious about God's work, he is not without humor. He gave me a good laugh the day I called to ask if he'd let me interview him for *Mountain Folk*. I identified myself as his "girlfriend." Without hesitation, Kenneth retorted, "Which one?" He made me laugh, and he made me a happy woman when he said he would be part of this fifth book about the mountain people of Virginia. I am honored to write his story.

~·~

Kenneth Ray Fitzgerald was the third son born to Aubrey Jennings Fitzgerald and Ethel Ray Grant Fitzgerald, whose family lived on Irish Creek. His grandparents on his father's side were Howell Gilbert Fitzgerald and Josephine Ramsey Fitzgerald. Kenneth can't recall the names of his mother's parents, but he remembers that Ethel's father carried the mail for many years. The six Fitzgerald children, by order of birth, were: twins Elmer and an unnamed brother who died at birth on August 9, 1926; Kenneth on June 20, 1928; Charlie in 1930; Rita in 1942; and Diane in 1943.

Kenneth started out life on Painter Mountain, near the little hamlet of Montebello. He was born in the "red house" that belonged to Frank and Deanie Humphreys, who had built and moved into another home on Painter Mountain. After the Fitzgeralds left the house that was painted red, the family lived in a two-story log house, then a railroad shanty in the same area.

The shanty was situated close to the tracks of the dinky railroad line that wound its way through the mountains and was used to haul cut timber to the South River Lumber Company near Buena Vista. Kenneth recalls that the train also carried groceries to people living in remote areas along the railroad. An order was written and given to someone riding the train to Buena Vista. The order was then taken to a store, filled, and put back on the train to be delivered.

Kenneth laughs at the memory of young Lyle Bradley, who was given the job of staying with the groceries once they were unloaded to make sure that the right people got their foodstuffs. "He had this dog, and it ran off down the hill and treed something. Lyle went to see about him and when he did, the hogs got into the groceries. Lyle said it was the last time they put him in charge of watching the groceries."

Aubrey Fitzgerald was a farmer and also cut timber for a living. Later, he found employment on the Blue Ridge Parkway as a maintenance worker. Those were the days when men knew the meaning of hard physical work. Trees were felled with crosscut saws, rocks were loaded by hand onto trucks and hauled to the rock crusher, and grass along the scenic road was cut with a mowing scythe. Aubrey eventually retired from the Park Service after many years.

Schoolchildren at the Montebello School

As a child, Kenneth attended the Montebello School, which was located at the top of Painter Mountain. It was a large, two-room building with an auditorium in the back. Some of Kenneth's classmates were Doris Cash, Lois Layton, and Elizabeth and Georgia Humphreys. When asked if he could remember some of his former teachers, Kenneth said, "I can remember the last one when I got up and quit!"

This was a provocative statement, so after we got finished

laughing, I prodded him for more information. "I quit in the fifth grade, and I can remember it like it was yesterday. My teacher was Mr. Whitehead from Lovingston, and he had a habit of falling asleep during class. We boys would sneak quietly behind him and scrape chalk dust into his hair, and when he'd wake up, he'd scratch his head and the dust would fall out on his desk.

"Once, he caught me throwing spitballs. He went up and wrote on the chalkboard, *I will not throw spitballs*, and told me to write that sentence, and when I got the board full, I could erase it and do it again. I went up to the board and think I wrote it twice and thought to myself, uh-uh. I remember turning around and picking up the chalk and eraser and walking up to his desk and saying to him, 'Sir, do you mind to do these until I come back?' I walked right on out and nobody said a word; you could have heard a pin drop.

"I came home, and Dad said, 'What are you doing home from school?' I said, 'I quit.' He told me, 'No you didn't,' and we argued back and forth, but in the end I won."

He was about nine years of age at the time he quit school, so Kenneth went to work alongside his father, cutting poplar trees on one end of a cross-cut saw, at a place called the "racetrack," deep in the mountains at the edge of Piney River. He remembers watching his uncle Willis's team of horses pull the logs out of the woods to be loaded onto trucks bound for the lumber mill his uncle, Manley Fitzgerald, owned in Fairfield.

"One time, they brought a guy in to cut logs with an old-fashioned power saw, and I never will forget Daddy saying, 'He thinks he's smart, don't he?' Uncle Willis told him, 'Well he's going to beat you all, because he can put out more logs than you do.' Dad walked up in the woods and started cutting and asked me, 'Are we going to let him beat us?' I said no, and I remember cutting trees, and we got so hot that my nose started to bleed, but we never let him get ahead of us. Every time he hit the ground with one, we'd lay one down next to his."

This reminded me of the song, "John Henry," about a man who laid down railroad tracks by sheer muscle power as fast as a machine could do it. Kenneth said that they worked at this location for about a year and a half, walking in and out, because they had no vehicle at the time.

"We never thought one thing about it. Walking never bothered me at all. Sometimes we'd walk to school in snow up to our knees, and our britches legs would be solid ice, and we'd have to stand by the side of the big old potbellied stove to thaw out.

"Later, Tom Byers drove a bus that would pick up the children, and sometimes he'd pull tricks on us. Like he'd make the bus jerk and come to a stop at the foot of the hill and tell us kids we'd have to get off so the bus could make it to the top. We'd all walk up the hill, and then he'd drive right up and say, 'Okay, now we can go.' But we got wise to him and whenever he pulled that trick, us kids would just sit there and tell him he'd just have to turn around and take us back home."

About a year later, on August 31, 1938, when he had just turned ten, Kenneth's mother died from complications after thyroid surgery. He remembers her being laid out in a casket in his home and having the funeral at Mount Paran Baptist Church, where the family attended. She is buried just inside the gate of the church cemetery, right next to the grave of her infant son who had died in 1926.

After Ethel passed away, Carrie Bell Moran Phillips was hired to help watch the children, and a year later, Aubrey and Carrie married. Carrie had a son named Eugene from her first marriage to Sylvester Hall Phillips. Eugene was eight years older than Kenneth, but Kenneth said that he never acted like some older teens who didn't want their little brothers hanging around. "He would let me go with him wherever he went and was always so nice to me. In many ways, he was closer to me than my own brothers. He died at Iwo Jima, Japan, during World War II, and is buried at Arlington National Cemetery."

Kenneth stayed at home until he was around sixteen years old. At that time, he found work at a furniture factory in Staunton, and stayed with an aunt who lived there. "I worked there until I met a man by the name of Sam Barton, who was in construction work, and he offered me a job. We hit it off, and he became just like a father to me.

"We built the Staunton post office and later went to Front Royal where we built a hospital, an addition onto a high school, and another school in Riverton. I could do just about anything: pour cement and finish it, as well as rough carpenter work. I met my wife, Mary Caroline Robinson, while working in Front Royal."

Sam was later diagnosed with cancer, and after he passed away, Kenneth found employment with another company that had also been working on the hospital and moved to Richmond. While in Richmond, Kenneth received a piece of paper in the mail stating, "Uncle Sam Wants You," and he was drafted into the army at the age of twenty-four.

The Korean War was still going on when Kenneth started basic training at Camp Pickett, just outside Richmond. Right before he finished basic, Mary and Kenneth were married by Rev. Russell Butcher at the Presbyterian Church in Hagerstown, Maryland, on November 1, 1952. Kenneth looked handsome in his army uniform, and Mary was a beautiful bride wearing a frilly dress. Kenneth said, "It was just me, Mary, the pastor, and the cleaning lady, who was our witness."

After he finished basic training, Kenneth was stationed in San Francisco, California, and Mary moved there to be with him after a few months. While in boot camp, the troops had been given eight weeks of infantry and eight weeks of training to be a medic; Kenneth's company drew the medic card. His first assignment was working as a corpsman at Leatherman Army Hospital.

The patients at the hospital were wounded men coming back from Korea. Kenneth was in charge of a ward of these men, helping them with bathing, transporting them in wheelchairs to different appointments, and generally doing anything else that needed to be done. He was stationed there for two years.

Their first child, Kenneth Ray Fitzgerald, Jr. ("Sonny"), was born in California on April 18, 1954. Kenneth's tour was up, and they left for Virginia in June of the same year. Kenneth worked a variety of jobs, including cab driver, before realizing that the army provided a better way of life, so he re-upped.

"I went and talked to the recruiter, and he asked if I knew anything about Fort Jackson, South Carolina, and I told him no, but I guess I could learn." He continued as a medic, often driving an ambulance or going out on training exercises.

Mary moved there with the baby after about a year, since on-base housing was limited at that time. The Fitzgeralds stayed at Fort Jackson for about four years; then Kenneth was shipped to Germany where they stayed for three years. During that time, their daughter, Teresa Elizabeth, was born on December 19, 1959, but she only lived five months before passing away on May 9, 1960. They brought their infant daughter back to the mountains of Virginia to be buried in the Mount Paran Church cemetery, then returned to Germany.

Kenneth and Mary shortly after their marriage

A year or so later, the family moved back to South Carolina, and their last child, Kevin, was born February 20, 1962, the same day that John Glenn went into orbit. From Fort Jackson, Kenneth was then sent to Korea, where the medic troops set up tents to take care of the incoming wounded, much like the popular TV show, M*A*S*H. He helped in the surgical unit and said that the doctors operated on the Korean people, too, many of whom were children whose parents could not afford medical care.

Kenneth served in Korea for a year and three months before being shipped back stateside to Fort Belvoir in Alexandria, Virginia. There he worked in the hospital OR and the recovery and emergency rooms. Here Kenneth began a year of schooling to become an army nurse. At this time, he was classified as an E-6 and volunteered to do a stint in Saigon, Vietnam in 1969.

There he helped to load weapons onto tanks for convoys in the field, or he would fly with the helicopter pilots over certain areas to take pictures of hidden Vietnamese bunkers. They would call in the information, and troops would then go out to these bunkers and remove all the weapons before blowing up the bunkers. Kenneth was in Vietnam for about a year before transferring to Fort Sam Houston in Texas. There, he worked at the burn center for two years. In 1972, after twenty-one years, he retired from the army with the rank of Sergeant First Class.

"We came back to Alexandria, where I worked in the civilian hospital for a few years, and then I met this major who introduced me to a colonel who offered me more money to come to the hospital at Fort Belvoir working civil service. I stayed until 1996, with almost forty-two years of combined years of service at my retirement."

I asked Kenneth if he enjoyed having a military career, and he said that he not only loved the work, but it gave him the chance to further his education and take college courses. He was happy to have the opportunity to learn more since that fateful day he quit school in Mr. Whitehead's fifth-grade class.

Over the years, Kenneth and Mary had come back to the mountains to visit their kinfolk. Kenneth, who has loved to hunt since he was a young boy, made the trips during hunting season so that he could deer hunt.

The decision was made to move back to Montebello when Kenneth's

Kenneth with a nice six-pointer

sister Rita became ill. Their father, Aubrey, who owned the property next to where Rita lived, died on November 26, 1968, at sixty-three years of age. He and his second wife, Carrie, were living on Zink's Mill School Road at the time. Carrie passed away on September 4, 1974, and is buried with Aubrey in the Haines Chapel Cemetery on South Mountain.

From Wilson Grant, Kenneth and Mary bought an acre of land that was located next to Rita's place and had a home built on the property. The couple continued to live there after Rita passed away in 1998, and Kenneth has stayed there since the death of his wife, Mary, on August 5, 2002. It is a cozy, happy

The Fitzgeralds in later years

home, filled with photographs and mementoes of a life well lived.

Kenneth is still very close to his last surviving sibling, Diane Ramsey, who lives in Prince Frederick, Maryland, and Kenneth currently has three grandchildren: Mary Kate, Jackie, and Colin and one great-granddaughter, Emmylou Grace Conner. His son Kevin lives in Alexandria, Virginia, and Sonny lives in Charlottesville, but he is planning to retire in 2015 and move back to the mountains to live with his dad. They are both looking forward to this.

Kenneth with his sons, Sonny and Kevin

Kenneth, at eighty-six years of age, is a busy man, who tends a garden, does his own canning, and continues to be active at Mount Paran Baptist Church. My husband, Billy, who was the pastor at the church for seven years, had the privilege of baptizing Kenneth in 2002 in the beautiful Tye River across the road from Evergreen Christian Church, where most of the mountain people prefer to be baptized.

You can always find Kenneth visiting the sick and shut-ins, helping to cut firewood, or running errands for nearly everyone he comes into contact with. He's

Kenneth with his sons and his sister Diane

Kenneth celebrating his birthday with Doris Cash for their 143 combined years

been this way ever since we've known him, and I asked if he'd learned this way of life from his parents.

"I can remember going with my dad to help someone build a shed, and when it was finished, they shook hands with never any money exchanged. But when he was in need, the same man would come to lend a hand without a thought of payment. People helped each other a lot more back then."

Billy Coffey baptizing Kenneth in 2002

Building a ramp at Dodie Robertson's

As we ended our conversation, I wondered why a man who had traveled the world would come back to Montebello, where he'd started out so many years ago. Kenneth's words struck a chord that I understood completely as he said with much emotion, "The mountains, ah the mountains; they call you back."

Splitting wood for the Campbell family

Mary and Kenneth (foreground) at Maxie Seaman's birthday party

Kenneth today, working in his garden

Frances May Hudson Fitzgerald

5

Frances May Hudson Fitzgerald

Anyone traveling on Route 56 through the village of Tyro is familiar with the Mountain View "Tea Room," which has been a landmark for many years and is the last country store of its kind in that area. Frances Fitzgerald has been the proprietor of the Tea Room for more than half a century and has a wealth of information and memories of people who have come and gone through the door over the years.

The Mountain View Tea Room

She lives in the back of the store, making it easy to keep house and cook meals in between customers. For the last five years, in the fall months, Frances has also worked at Tommy Fitzgerald's apple orchard just up the road on Harper's Creek; she opens the Tea Room from 5:30 p.m. until 9:00 p.m. in case anyone needs to pop in for some last-minute items.

When asked about the store's unique name, Frances explains that the former owner, Inez Taliaferro, thought up the title. Inez had a little snack bar where folks could buy hot sandwiches, cold drinks, or a cup of tea and sit down to enjoy it. Since the store already had a name people were familiar with, she decided to keep it once she and her husband bought the business and began running it as a general store.

Looking around the Tea Room evokes a time in history that is start-

The familiar Tea Room sign

ing to fade. Walls and ceiling are paneled in the old beadboard siding that was very popular in homes, churches, and stores a hundred years ago. Shelves line the walls, displaying canned food, old oil lamps, and a variety of household items for sale. A large wood stove occupies the rear of the store where folks can sit and warm themselves in the winter months. Frances said that a long bench used to sit next to the stove and was usually filled with local people visiting with each other.

A covered pool table dominates the middle of the floor; it serves as not only a gaming table but a catch-all for a little of everything, and sometimes it is a changing table for babies. The Tye River runs to the rear of the store, and a breathtaking view of Priest Mountain, the tallest in our area at 4,063 feet, can be seen from the front porch.

View of Priest Mountain from the Tea Room porch

Frances hosted a book signing at the Tea Room for my third book, *Backroads; Faces of Appalachia,* and I brought a lemon pound cake for refreshments. We had a good time talking to the folks we knew from that side of the mountain. I told Frances that we needed to repeat that for *Mountain Folk* so that she could sign autographs as well. I just might make another lemon pound cake and bring it!

There are certain people who are handpicked to work with the public. Frances Fitzgerald is one of those, a quiet-spoken woman genuinely interested in others. She has a listening ear and gentle humor, making her the perfect storekeeper to keep folks coming back. When she said yes to my request for an interview, it made my day! So fix yourself a cup of coffee, set right down, and enjoy Frances's story.

Frances May Hudson was the first child born to Scott Edward Hudson and Sally Stevens Hudson. The Hudsons had six children, and their order of birth was: Frances, who came into the world on April 14, 1937; Mary; Scott, Jr.; Joyce and Josephine, who were twins; and baby brother, Lewis. All six siblings still survive.

Dr. Dickie delivered Frances and her sister Mary, and he was the one who named both girls. "Mama said as soon as the baby was born and cleaned up, he'd give it a name; he didn't give the parents time to give it a name."

Frances's father, Scott, was from the Lovingston area of Nelson County, and the family moved around as he found various kinds of work. At the time of Frances's birth, the family was living in Massies Mill. Scott was a farmer and found work at a farm in Freshwater Cove owned by Mr. Fortune. After that, Scott took a job in Piney River at the American Cyanamid plant, which produced titanium oxide for use in making paint, among other things.

When Frances was school age, and while the family still lived in Freshwater Cove, she first attended the school in Lovingston. Later, the Hudson family rented a big white house belonging to Bill Boling that was on Route 56, directly across from where J&K country grocery now stands, so Frances began attending the Fleetwood School in Massie's Mill.

She remembers that some of her first teachers were: Minnie Dodd, who taught the second grade: Ruth Anderson, who was her third-grade teacher; and Mrs. Webb, who taught the fourth grade. Frances couldn't quite remember who her fifth-grade teacher was but said that Mrs. Turpin taught the sixth grade. She went to Fleetwood through the tenth grade, then the older children were bused to a new high school on Route 29.

Before the new school was built, which consolidated three area schools, there was Fleetwood, Lovingston, and Rockfish, all of which had eleven grades. Frances played softball and basketball, and all three schools played against one another in tournament games. Frances finished up the eleventh and twelfth grades at Nelson County High School and graduated in 1957.

I asked if anyone in the family played musical instruments, and Frances said no, but "I'll tell you a little story. When we were little and Mama would be busy cooking or doing something, Daddy had an old guitar, and he would take us out on the porch to play and sing for us. We thought he could really play, but when we got older, we'd ask him to get his guitar and sing, and he told us he never could play, he just strummed it to keep us kids entertained. He couldn't play the guitar, he was just playing at it!"

In the early years, before the family had access to electricity, Frances said that they lit oil lamps in the evenings for light. Sometime later, they hooked up to the electric lines coming through the county, and she can remember the family's first washing machine. "It was a Maytag that after the clothes had been washed, you fed them through a wringer and put them in rinse water."

As the children grew, they all helped with work around the house, but when Frances was around eight years old, she became the babysitter for all her younger siblings. "Mama

Frances at seventeen years of age

would work outside, feeding the chickens and milking the cow, and she'd sit me in the rocking chair with a baby on each leg and tell me to rock them until she came back."

Frances said she always was fond of horses, and her daddy had a gray workhorse named Nancy that Frances and her siblings used to ride bareback. "She was so gentle and good. We'd walk down in the field, put the bridle on her, and bring her up to the gate to get on her. Daddy would want to work her, but Nancy wouldn't let him catch her, so he'd say, 'One of you children go get her.'

"He plowed with her and pulled logs out of the woods. My brother would ride her to the mountains to get the harness hooked up so she could start pulling the logs out to the landing. She'd wait patiently until he'd unhook her, then ride her back up the mountain again. When Daddy had to sell her, all us children cried."

When Frances was a teenager, she and several family members worked in Turpin's peach orchard in Lovingston. Frances said that she worked in the packing shed doing whatever they asked her to do. "I was what you'd call a 'gofer' . . . go for this, go for that."

I asked Frances how she'd met her future husband, Austin Fitzgerald, Jr., who was always known by his nickname "Junie Bug." She said that their bus driver, Parrish Strickland, had told the boy to come down and ask her for a date. Frances laughed and said, "I told Junie Bug that Parrish was the one who got him in trouble!"

The date consisted of going over to Lovingston and having dinner at Joe Lee's Restaurant. Subsequent dates were going to the movies at the theater in Lovingston or to dances held at the large hall located next to the courthouse. Back then, movies were mostly westerns, and the dances had live music instead of DJs.

Junie Bug's parents were Austin Fitzgerald, Sr., and Florence Lawhorne Fitzgerald, who lived up Harper's Creek. Austin's daddy was Pat Fitzgerald, who lived on Coxes Creek.

Junie Bug, who was born on February 6, 1934, was three years older than Frances. He had enlisted in the military before they started to date and had served in Germany before being discharged in September 1957, three months before they married on December 7. The Fitzgeralds were married by Rev. Francis at the Presbyterian manse in Massies Mill. Witnesses

Four generations of Fitzgeralds: (top row) Bobby, Frances, and David Fitzgerald; (bottom row) Austin, Jr., Austin, Sr., and Pat

were Mrs. Francis and Miss Sanford, who was a school teacher who boarded with the Francises'.

After Frances and Austin, Jr., were married, they lived with his parents on Harper's Creek for about a year. Junie Bug worked with his father cutting timber; later he worked with Harold Campbell, who had a hauling business.

The Fitzgeralds started in the cattle business when Junie Bug and his father went to the livestock market, hoping to buy some steers to fatten and sell in the fall. When Austin, Sr., saw a nice lot of six Black Anguses come into the ring, he urged his son to bid on them. Junie Bug bought them but discovered as they were being loaded that they were heifers (female) rather than steers.

Austin said, "No matter, they will make you good cows." They continued in the cattle business from that time on, raising Black Angus as well as Charolaise, a pure white animal that was Junie Bug's favorite.

By then, Austin, Sr., had bought a home known as the "old Tice place," which was located up Battery Hill Road. He gave it to his son, and the young couple did some much-needed repairs before moving into their first home. At the time, Frances was working at Rayless Department Store in Lynchburg, and Junie Bug had found permanent employment at Morton Frozen Foods in Crozet. When their first son, Austin David, was born on July 12, 1960, Frances continued to work. When their second son, Bobby Wayne, came along on July 27, 1963, Frances quit her job and became a full-time mother.

When the boys were three and ten months old, respectively, the Fitzgerald family bought the Tea Room from Mrs. Taliaferro's daughter in March 1964, and Frances began a new career as a storekeeper.

At that time, there were several other country groceries in the Tyro area. Junior and Margie Hatter ran one farther up the mountain, and Byron and Louise Bradley had a store just up the road. Below the Tea Room, Captain Billy Massie ran a store that also housed the Tyro post office. When Massie's store closed, Byron and Frances both put in bids for the postal office, but Byron's

Junie Bug and young David

David's fifth birthday: (top row) Frances, Bobby, Junie Bug, and Florence Fitzgerald; (bottom row) David and cousins Danny and Karen Stevens

bid was lower, so the post office went to his store. There were no hard feelings, as Frances told me, "With two small children underfoot and all the people coming in and out to buy things, I had my hands full."

The Tea Room had hours from seven in the morning until nine at night Monday through Friday; it closed at six on Saturday evenings so that the family could have a little time together. On Sundays, it opened after church and remained open until nine. The hours have stayed the same except in the fall, when Frances works at Fitzgerald's Orchard, so she doesn't open until five thirty.

Frances used to attend church at the Tyro Presbyterian Chapel, directly behind the Tea Room, but after that church closed, she began going to Harmony Presbyterian Church, just up the road a mile or two from the Tea Room. Frances's son David and his wife, Sherry, restored the old church and now live and raised their two children, David Austin II and Alexandra Dean, there. Bobby Wayne lives in another house on the property, and Frances raised his daughter, Tasha, "As one of my own."

Austin Fitzgerald family portrait

I asked if there was enough business to support four stores in just a few miles stretch, and Frances explained, "Before Lovingston started to build up with the new Food Lion and Dollar General store, this little hollow was a booming place, because everybody did their whole week's shopping in these little stores."

Although she didn't carry a line of fresh meats, the Tea Room had lunch meats, such as ham and bologna, and the big wheels of "rat cheese" in wooden boxes that most country stores kept sitting on the counter. Dettor, Edwards & Morris, a company in Crozet, and Callahan out of Lynchburg were the wholesale food vendors who serviced the Tea Room. Other companies wholesaled hardware and novelty items, as well as bread, milk, and snacks. Frances said the Tea Room carried Monticello Ice Cream that, in her opinion, "Was the best you can buy!"

People who popped in on a regular basis were Daniel Lawhorne, Icem and Peggy Lawhorne, Clemon and Peggy Lawhorne, Lester and Sylvia Allen, and Corine Painter from Massies Mill. Also in years past, a lot of passers-through, hikers walking the Appalachian Trail from Georgia to Maine, would trek the two miles off the trail down to the Tea Room to stock up on high-energy foods. Today, Frances said that she doesn't get as many trail hikers because they have learned that they can stop in the town of Buena Vista, south of Tyro, and pack enough food to hold them to the next big town of Waynesboro.

Junie Bug, as well as many of his family members, have always been big hunters, and the Tea Room was a local hangout for those who brought in deer, turkey, and bear. It was also the place where the hunters gathered in the morning to map out where they were going that day. Bear hunting has been, and continues to be, one of the most popular sports in Nelson County, especially for the men living in the mountains.

Frances said that Dave Hatter used to regularly come into the store. He would tell her boys long-winded stories while she was working, which really helped entertain them. Even though the Tea Room is located right on Route 56, Frances said she never had a problem with either one of the boys going out into the road. She recalls that when Bobby Wayne was a little boy, he would sit in his playpen and stick his legs out the slats. He would pull himself and the playpen along the floor over to where the Zesta crackers were kept and open the package.

Tyro bear hunters: (top row) James Lewis Mays, Warren Mays, Danny Stevens, John Henry Fitzgerald, and Junior Evans; (middle) Wickey Stevens, Glen Fitzgerald, and Davis Newton; (kneeling) Daniel Lawhorne and Junie Bug Fitzgerald

"Every morning, you could bet he'd work his way over to those crackers. He wouldn't eat them, he'd just rip open the box. I would smack his little hands and pull him back, and he wouldn't fool with them anymore for that day. But the next morning, he'd be right back. About the third time he did it, I got the switch I kept for David, and I kind of switched his little legs, and from that time on, he never fooled with them crackers anymore!"

Bobby Wayne never lost his adventurous spirit, but when he was eighteen years old, he was in a serious motorcycle accident close to home. His right arm was injured so

The "Little Tyro Bear Hunters"

severely that it had to be amputated, but Frances said that he adjusted to losing his limb and continues to help his brother with the farm work.

Another "disaster" the family suffered happened when Bobby Wayne was just six. Frances recalls the harrowing night of August 19, 1969, when Hurricane Camille ripped through Nelson County, causing major loss of life as well as property. She recalls not only the torrential rain but the near-constant lightning that lit up the night sky. She was thankful that her daddy had asked to take the kids back home with him to Shipman earlier in the day, because she hadn't been sure that she and her husband would survive the flood that covered the land where they lived.

The Fitzgeralds had gone to bed around eleven o'clock and hadn't realized just how much the water was surrounding the Tea Room until Junie Bug mentioned that the roof was leaking. Frances got a pan to put under the stream of dripping water.

"I laid back down again and dozed off to sleep for about thirty minutes before Junie Bug said, 'Frances, that pan is running over.' I always put a flashlight under my pillow, since the children were little, so I flashed it over to where the pan was, and then got up and noticed my feet were wet; the water was coming into the store from the kitchen. I walked to the windows and looked out with my flashlight and saw the water was level with the windows. Luckily I didn't try to open the front door, or I think the water would have exploded the house.

"Knowing we were surrounded, I asked Junie Bug what were we going to do, and he said the only thing we could do was to ride it out. So we climbed up into the attic and stayed there until morning. All night long, we could hear things falling off the shelves in the store. At daybreak, Junie Bug cut a hole in the gable end of the house so he could see out and noticed Odell Lawhorne's car was sitting out in the field. Odell lived on the road above us, and Junie Bug said he had probably washed away in the flood.

"When we finally came down from the attic, we were in mud up to our knees. We went outside, and Junie Bug and some others walked up to where Odell lived and found him hanging in a tree. Odell climbed down and, as they were walking back, noticed something that looked like a doll tangled up in the debris. They went to see about it and found Ashby Statton's daughter, who had washed down the river, and they took her body back to the church.

"A helicopter flew over, and we waved a white dishrag, but he didn't land; he was just flying over to scout out who needed help. A bunch of men got a rope and were on the opposite side of the river, and they wanted us to get into a tub so they could pull us over. I told them I couldn't swim, and if that tub turned over, I'd be gone! But they cut a big tree that had fallen over a telephone line to the other side, and I told them I would walk across if someone would hold onto me. We walked over to the other side and up over the mountain to Mr. Fitzgerald's house on Harper's Creek."

Junie Bug's brother, John Henry, and his family lived just below the Tea Room, and Frances said that the flood had washed part of their house away. John Henry and his wife, Frances, had climbed into the attic with their son, J. H., who was just a few months old.

"They had J. H. in a little bassinette next to their bed, and when they woke up and realized the water was inside the house, the bassinette had already floated into the living room and never tipped over, because Frances had put a piece of plastic under the baby mattress which acted like a boat. God does work in miraculous ways, because if the basket had gotten into the main stream of water and floated to the back of the house, he would have washed away."

Frances said that it took about a month to get everything cleaned up, and people from the Mennonite churches around the area came to help people get back to normal. "I was out back, trying to clean clothes, and Junior was gone to try and get us another vehicle, since ours had washed away, when this Mennonite man came up to me and said, 'Young lady, do you need any help?' I told him I wouldn't mind it, so he left and when he came back, he had a whole truckload of people who came and helped us clean the mud off the furniture and anything else that had to be done."

Frances said that although she wasn't really scared, whenever it rained hard after that, she and her family would seek shelter at the Roseland Rescue Squad, "Just as a precaution; to be on the safe side." I know many people in Nelson County who still feel the emotional impact of Hurricane Camille's damage to this day.

After the flood: August 19, 1969

When the Fitzgeralds first got married, Junie bug had contracted pneumonia, and it settled in one of his lungs. The doctor told him that he'd need an operation to take out the diseased portion of the lung if he was to make it. He had the operation, but a blood clot formed in his

The devastation from Hurricane Camille

leg, and Frances said that it always gave him trouble after that. Later he developed heart problems, and, ultimately, that's what took his life in 1998.

That was more than sixteen years ago, but Frances, in her matter-of-fact way, says, "You accept the idea and try to move on. There's no turning back, you just have to go forward." People wondered if she would keep the store after her husband died, and Frances told them, "He's gone, and I have to live my life until my toes are sittin' up!"

Frances, who is now seventy-seven, continues to be the proprietor of the Tyro Tea Room. When she's not waiting on customers, she says that she loves to read. Her two sons live just outside her back door if she needs help, and she still attends Harmony Presbyterian Church. Her grandson Austin lives at home and works locally; granddaughters Alexandra and Tasha have jobs and live elsewhere. Tasha is in the process of adopting two children, Christopher, age five, and Hailey, two. When the adoption is final, Frances will have two new branches added to her family tree.

Frances Fitzgerald in her Tyro store

So this is the story of Frances May Hudson Fitzgerald, a soft-spoken woman, a keeper of the faith, and an encourager to anyone coming through the front door of Tyro's Tea Room.

Marvin Samuel Henderson

6

Marvin Samuel Henderson

My friendship with Marvin and his family goes back to the early 1970s, before I actually moved to the community of Love. Our family used to come up and visit Sonny and Bunny Stein, who lived a little farther up the mountain from the Hendersons. Several times, the Steins took us down to Marvin's house, where people were gathered inside their garage, making music, dancing, and generally having a good time. Little did I know I'd end up singing with Marvin once I moved here permanently.

Marvin's wife, Jean, remembers that on one occasion, I had made some sassafras tea and brought it along. Marvin remembers my hair, which was styled at the time in a larger-than-life 'fro of gigantic proportions. I never lived down that hairdo.

What I remember most about Marvin is that he is so funny! Always smiling, never in a bad mood. He has a quick wit. He will say things like, "It takes longer to walk out and get the newspaper than it does to read it," poking fun at how short on news the paper is. Whenever someone wanted him to play and sing the anniversary song, he'd say, "We will now play 'Faded Love.'" Or when his boss told him they didn't have too much work for him, he'd reply, "Oh, that's okay; it doesn't take too much work for me anyway."

He made me a happy woman when he said yes to my request of letting me interview him for *Mountain Folk*, because he, my husband, and Marvin's cousin, Bobby Henderson, are the last three Love natives still living in the same place they started out. In talking with Marvin, I learned so much about the early days here on the mountain, and for those of you reading Marvin's chapter, you will learn it, too. Enjoy the read!

❦

Marvin's grandparents on his father's side were Robert and Lena Henderson, who lived one ridge over on a farm on Reeds Gap. On his maternal side were Sidney Quick and Minnie Truslow Quick. The Quicks lived less than a mile down the road from where Marvin lives now.

Marvin's parents were Odie Trelawney Henderson and Hallie Frances Maybelle Quick Henderson. Hallie's people were from Nelson County, and that is where she was born on September 26, 1910, one of eleven children. Odie, born September 16, 1902, was of the Mennonite faith, and he and Hallie were

Marvin's grandparents, Sidney and Lena Henderson

members of Mountain View Mennonite Church their whole married lives. Both are buried in the church cemetery. Mountain View is located at the foot of the mountain where Love Road and Reeds Gap converge.

When Odie and Hallie were first married on June 23, 1927, they lived in a home close to where Hallie's parents lived, and their first two sons were born there. Joseph Wilson Henderson came first on March 10, 1928, and Melvin Odie was next on October 9, 1936. Later, the family moved to the little roadside home of Hallie's parents, and Marvin Samuel, the youngest of their three sons, was born there on August 29, 1940.

Marvin's father, Odie, died of a heart attack at home on October 4, 1941, when Marvin was only thirteen months old. Odie was working on the Blue Ridge Parkway at the time and had worked that day feeling fine, but he died in his sleep later that night. Hallie never remarried after Odie passed away.

Marvin's father, Odie Trelawney Henderson

I remember talking with Hallie back in the 1980s, and she said that a lot of people told her at the time to let others raise the boys, because she wouldn't be able to feed them. Hallie, who was one of the most feisty, independent women I've ever met, told them that if they starved, they'd all starve together, but she would find a way to keep her family intact! It was just a short time afterward that

Hallie found work at the Stelhi Silk Mill in Waynesboro, producing enough of an income to raise all three of her boys. Later, the mill was bought out by another factory that made blankets.

Although Hallie did not drive, Guy Hewitt, who lived up the mountain, worked at the same factory, and he would pick up Hallie for work, then bring her home in the evenings. While Hallie was working, her brother Sidney watched over the boys. They lived in the house where Marvin was born until he was around eight years old. By that time, Hallie had saved up enough money to buy a home just up the road.

Marvin said that she paid three thousand dollars for the house and the three acres that came with it. The home had been built by Carl Hewitt, Sr., who got the lumber from the abandoned Dunkard Church at Love. Marvin thought that the house had originally had one floor, and the second story was added at a later time. After Carl left the house, he rented it to Saylor and Pearl Hatter, who had a large family, before eventually selling it to Hallie.

Hallie on the porch of her home (1982)

Even after they moved to the new home, Marvin said that his Uncle Sid walked up to visit each day, and he continued to do so until his health prohibited it. This was a time when people didn't knock on the door but walked right on in; a time when apples were kept in a sack under the bed and were brought out when people came to visit.

Marvin's wife, Jean, said, "Everyone sat around peeling apples and eating them while they talked." This practice was still ongoing when I moved here in 1980. My husband, Billy, said that apples were given instead of the contemporary piece of cake and a cup of coffee. I can remember going to Forest and Eva Coffey's house and having them offer me an apple.

The home where Marvin grew up as it is now

Oh the times I watched Forest's brother, Johnny Coffey (my first neighbor), sit with a metal dishpan on his lap, peeling a whole apple with a knife, never once tearing the skin. When he had finished, he'd cut a slice and hand it to me. No matter how much I practiced, I never could get the hang of peeling an apple without breaking the rind. It was also at their house where I learned about the superstition of leaving through the same door in which you came.

Marvin said that he and his brothers had chores like every other child while growing up. They worked the garden, knowing that the food they grew meant survival. Hallie canned everything so that the family would have food to eat all year.

Marvin remembers, "My job was to bring two buckets of water from the spring to the house every evening after I got off the school bus. Then I had to come in and peel potatoes. We had potatoes every night. Melvin did all the cooking. We did a lot of hunting, because that was the only way we got any meat."

When asked what he hunted, Marvin said, "We'd go squirrel hunting, deer hunting, and occasionally we'd shoot a groundhog—anything that moved, really. That was a big feast for us! Let me tell you, we had close to nothing, but I thought everybody else lived that way, too, so we didn't know the difference."

He and Melvin were also in charge of getting in wood for heating and cooking. The boys would go up to the top of the ridge in front of their house, drag enough wood out for that night, and cut it up with a crosscut saw. With his typical humor, Marvin said, "I was eight years old before I realized my name was not 'Get Wood'!"

No one on the mountain had electricity or indoor plumbing at that time, so the boys did their homework by the light of oil lamps. In fact, Hallie lived without electricity until just a few years before she passed away on May 25, 1989, and she never did have indoor plumbing during her lifetime. Marvin said that she washed clothes on a scrubbing board in a washtub full of water brought in from the spring out back, but years later, she purchased a Maytag gas-powered wringer/washing machine that made her life easier.

The boys worked hard from an early age, but they had their share of fun, too. There was a deep swimming hole along Back Creek on the property of Marvin's cousin, Bobby Henderson, where a large waterwheel had provided power to heat two chicken houses owned by a Mr. Perry. Bobby said that the water traveled down a wooden trough from Back Creek and filled the metal slots on the overshot wheel, making it turn. The chicken houses were gone by the time he and Marvin swam in the hole, but the old waterwheel was still standing and can be seen in the photo below.

Bobby also said that, as children, they climbed up on the struts of the large waterwheel, making it turn slowly. He remembers that Amos Bridge later took the wheel down and sold the metal for scrap. Marvin said that during the summer, they swam every day. The photograph was taken by a man from West Virginia who was passing through, and it was later featured in a magazine. The picture was sent back to the families of the boys and shows—from left to right—Melvin, Marvin, Doug and Bobby Henderson, Floyd Quick, and Billy Henderson.

The swimming hole in Back Creek

Marvin said that they would also hike over the mountain to Sherando Lake and go swimming there as well. Marvin learned how (not) to sew from an experience he had at the swimming hole. "I tore my swimsuit and looked at it and thought, I can fix that! I went home and got on Mama's treadle sewing machine and stitched up where it was ripped. When I went to put them back on, I realized I had sewed up the leg along with the rip. That ended my sewing career!"

The Love Road was still dirt when Marvin was little and wasn't paved until sometime in the late 1940s. The original road differed from where it now lies, and if you look closely, you can still see parts of the old roadbed. Marvin remembers that his uncle, Sherman Quick, had one of the first cars he can remember seeing up here: a 1939 Ford.

Marvin started the first grade at six years of age at the Sherando School. His teacher was Jean Davies. The school closed at the end of that year, halfway through the term. So Marvin was then bused to Stuarts Draft, where he attended the remainder of first grade and grades two through five at the elementary school. He completed grades six and seven at another building next to the elementary school. Some of the other children that Marvin went to school with from the Love area were: Shelby Everitt, Billy Coffey, Roger and Hettie Hewitt, Bobby Henderson, JoAnn Henderson, and Leland Coffey.

Young Marvin on the Parkway

At that time, there was no eighth grade; after the students finished the seventh grade, they went to Wilson Memorial

Marvin's school picture (1948–1949)

Marvin's school picture (1950–1951)

High School in Fishersville for their freshman, sophomore, junior, and senior years. Marvin graduated in the class of 1957 at sixteen years of age, along with members of the famous Statler Brothers, who wrote a popular song called "Class of '57."

Upon graduation, Marvin got a job, carrying bricks and blocks and mixing mortar, with Sidney Shirley, a mason who lived in Sherando. Marvin worked for Sidney until he was eighteen and bought his first car: a red and white 1953 Ford Victoria.

A later school picture of Marvin

His next car was a 1956 Ford Victoria that Marvin said, "Would take you on down the road!" I asked if he liked to drive fast, and he replied, "I was reckless and wild and probably shouldn't even be here. All the boys around here loved

Marvin and his 1953 Ford Victoria

to race from here to Waynesboro. It was me, Joe Bridge, Donald Umbarger, and Bobby Henderson. Before we had cars, Bobby and I would start out walking to Waynesboro every Saturday night to go to the skating rink, and then walk home in the dark at two o'clock in the morning. We kept this road hot! Gene Everitt worked the night shift and got off at midnight, and if he saw us on the road, he'd pick us up on his way home."

The Henderson boys: Marvin, Joe, and Melvin

That was when there weren't too many houses, and Jean said, "You knew everybody from Love to Waynesboro. You weren't scared to be on that road, because you knew who lived in every house. Now you don't know who lives in any of them."

After Marvin left working for Sidney Shirley, he found employment as a truck driver at the Daylight Laundry in Waynesboro. Jean was working at Doctor Woods's office, and they met when Marvin came in for a delivery. Jean said that she had never seen anyone so shy, and it took a while before Marvin got up the nerve to ask her out.

When asked where they had gone on their first date, neither could remember, but Marvin said, "Probably Hamburger Franks." This was a hamburger stand in Waynesboro that didn't have pricing, just the slogan, "Pay what it's worth." Needless to say, Hamburger Franks was not in business all that long!

Jean Elizabeth Brooks was born on October 28, 1939, and grew up in Waynesboro. She graduated from high school in 1958. She was the daughter of Erskine Brooks and Eliza Lotts Brooks, whose family was from the Spottswood/Raphine area. Her father was employed at Rhames Jewelry Store as a jeweler, working on watches and clocks. Her mother was a nurse.

Marvin at that time had moved on from being a truck driver for Daylight Laundry and had found a job at the Early Dawn Dairy. Marvin and Jean dated "every night for two years," and married at the Waynesboro Christian Church on February 4, 1960. Marvin remembers that the preacher who married them was Roger Powell.

Marvin and Jean when courting

Marvin was handsome, dressed in the one suit he owned, and his pretty bride wore a street-length dress made of taffeta. The first place they lived was in a small apartment behind a large, white Victorian home on East Main Street. Marvin said, "We lived there for six months, and I told Jean, this city life is not for this ol' country boy, and I'm headed to the mountains. Six months is about five and a half months too long!"

They came to Love and moved in with Marvin's mother for several months before purchasing a modular home from Lee Wood Homes and erecting it on a piece of land that Hallie had given them across the road. She had given Melvin an adjoining piece of property, where Marvin's garden spot was located, and Marvin bought that land from his brother before

Melvin passed away in 2009.

Marvin remembers that the same day Lee Wood Homes started building the house was the same day that he got the call telling him that his grandmother, Lena Henderson, had died. It was October 20, 1961. After the shell of the home was built, the Hendersons did all the interior finish work, such as sheetrock and flooring, by themselves. They moved in by Christmas of the same year.

Christmas 1961: Marvin, Hallie, and Melvin

Their first child, Marvin Samuel Henderson, Jr. ("Junior"), had been born in June 1961, and their daughter, Cheryl, came four years later in January 1965. Jean said that because of distance, she didn't see as much of her side of the family as she did her husband's. Like the story of Ruth and Naomi in the Bible, Jean said, "His people became my people." Her mother passed away in 1977, her father in 1981, and both are buried at Riverview Cemetery in Waynesboro.

On April 1, 1964, Marvin went to work at the General Electric Company based in Waynesboro. He was an inspector and tester of the relays, aircraft parts, and printers that were manufactured there. He even worked on some of the parts that went into the space shuttle. GE was bought out by another company and renamed Genicom; Marvin had thirty-four years of service when he left in 1998, three months before the company closed. For another five years afterward, he commuted to Charlottesville to work as an inspector at National Optronics, a com-

A Henderson family portrait

pany that made eyeglass lenses and the machines used to cut them.

Jean stayed home to take care of the children until they were in high school, then she got a job sewing at Barksdale Furniture Company in Waynesboro. She sewed draperies, valances, and anything else they needed. Later, she did the same type of work for people out of her home. She had learned to crochet at ten years of age and had taken a sewing class in the eighth grade. She said that it was something she loved and always enjoyed. Jean is a very talented seamstress, and some of her applique quilting projects are truly works of art. She continues to make beautiful crocheted lap robes and did a lot of crocheted caps for babies and cancer patients who have lost their hair due to chemotherapy.

Jean showing some of her handwork

Marvin got his first guitar at sixteen years of age, when he began earning his own money working for Sidney Shirley. He said that he never took lessons; the music was just "in him," and he taught himself to play. He started out playing guitar with his brother, Melvin, and with friends, and he has been at it ever since. In recent years, Marvin has played at five different nursing homes each month, bringing a lot of joy to the residents. He's been at every party and pig roast here in the mountains, and in years past, he and Jean hosted music gatherings at their home that everyone came to and really enjoyed. He continues to play at the community bluegrass jams at Stuarts Draft Mennonite Church and the Sherando Ruritan Club.

New Year's Eve Service at Mountain View: (top row) Allan Swarey, Simon Kinsinger, and Marvin; (bottom row) Sylvia Swarey and Lynn Coffey (1982)

In 1982, while I was attending Mountain View Mennonite Church, Marvin talked me into singing with a bluegrass gospel group, consisting of myself, Marvin, Allan and Sylvia Swarey, and their cousin, Simon Kinsinger. We made our debut at the

Mountain View watch-night service on December 31, all dressed in bib overalls and red bandana–style shirts. When Marvin dug out the photo shown below, I about died laughing. Billy said that I looked like a teenager, but at the time I had just turned thirty-five years old. Oh, to be that age again!

We went on from there, adding different people to the bluegrass group we now called "Back Creek." We practiced in Marvin's garage, and we would sing at various places, such as Margie Hatter's homeplace over in White Rock, at different churches, and at the Sherando Lake amphitheater on Saturday nights.

So many memories. Jean said it right when she told me this interview was just as much for me as it was for them. From talking and visiting with Hallie while she was living, to waving to Marvin and Jean every time we passed by coming down the mountain, to watching their kids grow up from the teen years to married adults, we've done a lot of living together.

Junior Henderson married Vicki Hosaflook of Bridgewater on October 19, 1985, and their only child, a daughter named Stacie Ann, was born October 27, 1987. They reside in Stuarts Draft and are active members at Waynesboro Mennonite Church. Stacie lives with her parents and has two children from a former marriage, Elsie Ann and Caleb Michael.

Cheryl married David Glen "Buck" Morris, Jr., on May 11, 1996, and they live in Unionville, Virginia, and attend Roadsville Baptist Church.

Marvin is still full of good humor, and his repertoire of one-liners never ceases to make me laugh. However, I'd like to end by saying that the man also has a very tender heart. He took care of his mother until her dying day, mowing her yard and tending to her every need. When the recorder quit taping, Marvin told me a little story that shows exactly what I mean.

He said that while he and his friends were playing at the nursing homes, there was a ninety-six-year-old man by the name of Mr. James, who seemed to really enjoy the music.

Marvin and Jean at home

Mr. James had confided to Marvin that he used to play a little when he was younger. In talking a little more, Marvin found that Mr. James still had his guitar and kept it in his room. Marvin told the man to go get it so that he could play a little with them. Mr. James said that he didn't want to make them sound bad.

Marvin laughed and told him, "You can't make us sound any worse than we already are!"

The old man picked up his guitar and started to play. Marvin's eyes filled with tears as he told me that he had never seen such a radiant smile come over anyone and light up an entire room as it did the day Mr. James played his guitar. From then on, each time Marvin came to the nursing home where the man lived, Mr. James was always invited to play along.

This is the story of Marvin Samuel Henderson's life, and I, as his longtime friend and neighbor here in Love, have been honored to write and preserve it.

Marvin in a familiar pose with his guitar

Barbara Gormes and Peggy Ballowe

7

The Fitzgerald Sisters: Peggy Ballowe and Barbara Gormes

It's hard to pinpoint the exact time I first met the Fitzgerald sisters, because I've bumped into them at different times since moving here. I remember going over to Peggy's house back in 1982 to interview her daughter, Lisa, after she was attacked by a bear while walking in the woods. In 1983, the sisters' father, Raymond, wrote down his early memories of being born and raised in the mountains; in 1987, he sent his memoirs to *Backroads* newspaper. His story was published in the February, April, and May issues of the newspaper, and I included his story in the second Backroads book, *The Road to Chicken Holler*.

Gradually, I came to realize that the Fitzgeralds were related to my husband, Billy, in that Raymond was the first cousin of Billy's dad, Saylor, and their grandmother, Rose Ella Coffey Fitzgerald, was the sister of Billy's grandmother, Tressa Coffey Coffey. I'm not sure how that equates in the family tree, but we are certainly glad they are one of our branches.

The entire Fitzgerald clan has had an unusually close relationship, and through the years, most members have put down roots in the exact same spot in the community of Beech Grove that generations before have made their home. Read on as the Fitzgerald sisters take you on a trip back in time.

Peggy and Barbara's maternal grandparents were Russell and Leatha Harris, who lived in a place called Phoenix, close to the villiage of Norwood. Because of some unforeseen family dynamics, Peggy and Barbara's mother, Alice Bessie (born 1922), and Bessie's older sister, Katherine, were raised by another woman, "Big Bessie" Terry, who lived on top of Johnson/Terry Mountain near Roseland. Bessie was nine months old at the time the Terrys took her, and she stayed until she was nineteen, when she married Raymond Ralph Fitzgerald.

Peggy and Barbara's paternal grandparents were Napoleon "Po" Fitzgerald and his second wife, Rose Ella Coffey Fitzgerald, who lived in Beech Grove. Napoleon was married first to Katherine Blackwell, and they had eleven children together. "Po" and Rose Ella's family graced the front cover of the fourth Backroads book, *Appalachian Heart*.

The old weatherboard home shown in the photo burned down, and the sisters were told that their granny's second home, which was located down the road a short distance, was rolled up the mountain. Logs had been laid under the foundation, and a team of horses had pulled it to its new location. Napoleon and Rose Ella had five children: Hoy, Tucker, Raymond (born 1911), Effie, and Tommy, who are shown in the photograph with their parents.

I asked how Raymond and Bessie had met, since there was quite a distance between their homes. The sisters said that Bessie lived in a very remote area that did not even have a road to the home, just a "goat path" cut up the side of the mountain from the main road. Every Sunday, the family would walk down to the one-room Massie Memorial Baptist Church in Freshwater Cove for services. Raymond spent a lot of time at a friend's house at the bottom of the Cove, and he met Bessie at church. From that time on, Raymond courted his future wife, walking the steep path up to her home more times than he cared to remember.

The Fitzgerald Sisters: Peggy Ballowe and Barbara Gormes 101

Napoleon Fitzgerald's family

Barbara laughed as she recalled, "Daddy walked that mountain and walked that mountain and finally told Mama on his last trip, if she didn't marry him, he wasn't coming back!" The couple married in September 1941 in Charleston, South Carolina. "Mama had never been anywhere but on that mountain all of her life, and Daddy told her he would take her to get married somewhere she had never been before."

The newlyweds came back from their honeymoon

Raymond and Bessie (1948)

and moved in with Raymond's mother. Napoleon had died in 1922 when Raymond was just eleven years of age, so the move helped both Rose Ella and the young couple who were just starting out. The Fitzgeralds eventually had four children. Peggy came first, on June 8, 1942, and was born in the upstairs room of her grandmother's house. Rose Ella and her brother Tommy's wife, Ruth, were there to help with the delivery. Peggy's given name is Dorothy Mae, but she was always called Peggy.

Peggy and Barbara at their granny's house

Barbara Ruth came next on January 14, 1944. By then, Raymond had built a new house for his family right next to his mother's home, and that is where Barbara was born. Doctor Dickie was the attending physician at her birth.

David Lee ("Fuzzy") was born on November 24, 1946, at the University of Virginia hospital. When I asked how their brother got his nickname, Barbara explained that Caskie Fitzgerald and Raymond took David to the movie theater in Lovingston where a western was playing, and the star of the show was Fuzzy Jones. As a child, David's hair was just like cotton, it was so soft, and Caskie pinned "Fuzzy" on him. From that time on, the name stuck, and most people today don't know him by any other name.

Raymond Ralph, Jr., was the last to arrive, on November 29, 1948, and because he was the baby, many friends and family members still call him by his nickname, "Baby Ray." Raymond's brother Tommy and his wife, Ruth, lived on the upper side of Rose Ella and had three boys—Roger, Donald ("Dinky"), and Toby—who were more like brothers than cousins to Raymond's kids because of the close proximity of their homes.

(Back row) Peggy, Raymond, Fuzzy, Roger (on car), and Barbara; (front row) Dinky and Baby Ray

Peggy and Barbara remember that Uncle Tommy had all types of different jobs as they were growing up, including his own dry-cleaning business and selling pots and pans door to door.

The girls remember one winter when they were teenagers that they got a deep snow that stopped all vehicular traffic. Alvis Grant lived up the mountain from the Fitzgeralds, and his sons, Charles and "Duck," hooked up their team of horses to a large ground sled with a wood stove set in the middle, along with a supply of wood. They came down the road,

Barbara, Peggy, cousin Roger, and Josephine Terry by Tommy's car

picking up kids and taking grocery orders for those living on Beech Grove Road, and headed for Duncan's Store. There, the Duncans filled orders, marking who got what on various grocery tabs, before the boys headed back up the mountain to deliver people's items. Not only did the children have a fun winter outing, but thanks to the Grant's ingenuity, they kept warm, too!

Barbara also remembered that snow didn't stop the buses from running when she was in high school. "We would come home in snow storms. I remember one time we were on Adial Road coming from Lovingston, and the chains on the bus broke. Leo Ponton was our bus driver, and he got all the girls to take off their neck scarves and tie them together so he could tie the chains back on until we could make it home." Now they cancel school at the hint of a little snow.

The sisters started school at the Rockfish School in Greenfield, which had grades one through seven. The high school consisted of grades eight, nine, ten, and eleven. Mr. Lawman was the school principal. When asked who were some of the early teachers, Barbara said that Isabell Saunders was her first-grade teacher, Mrs. Flora Hughes taught both girls in the third grade, and Peggy volunteered that Emma Massie, at one time or another, taught nearly every student in Nelson County.

Margaret Garth taught the seventh grade, and when Mr. Lawman had to be away, she acted as assistant principal in his absence. Margaret also ran the Tuckahoe Tavern for many years, and it was a popular eating establishment in the Nellysford area. Years later, Peggy and her husband did all the maintenance work at the tavern, as well as at several other businesses Margaret owned.

People in the Beech Grove community besides the Fitzgeralds were: Clarence and Pearl Campbell, the Alvis Grants, and Morel and Jeanette Atkins, who operated a sawmill owned by William Maddox of North Carolina. The Atkins later moved back to North Carolina, and their land was bought by the Robert Mansfield family, who started and continue to run the Piney Mountain Bible Camp.

There were also families of Fields, Dodds, Hugheses, Duncans, and Thompsons in the small mountain community. Maphis Campbell's father, Marcellus, had a mill and apple-packing shed, and Peggy remembers that one time her father had gone down to get some apples from the Campbells, and Baby Ray climbed up on the conveyor machine, got caught in it, and had to be pulled out.

The sisters remember life before the main road was paved, saying, "We played in the middle of the road. There were probably five cars a day when people went to work and then came back home. In the early 1950s, Pearson Duncan drove a bus when the DuPont plant was booming that took people to work and back, and he turned around in Mama and Daddy's front yard before going back down the mountain. Their yard was even with the road back then, and there wasn't a bank. The terrain of the land changed after the '69 flood."

Peggy said, "We grew up all together, and our granny was the central part of our life. She was always giving us advice, and when we were hungry and wanted one of her good scrambled eggs, you'd run in her back door and say, 'Granny, scramble me an egg.' She'd get the fire going in the wood stove and got down her iron pan and would [cook] you the best egg you ever ate." Barbara added, "And those cornbread fritters!"

The girl's grandmother took them to church in the old one-room, weatherboard Beech Grove Christian Church, located where the Cub Creek

Barbara and Peggy, Fuzzy on the car (1951)

Cemetery now stands. They remember that Mr. Clarence Campbell was the church superintendent, and the preacher was a Mr. McKinney.

Barbara remembers, "Granny would take us to the revivals, and if you dozed off to sleep, she would tap you on the leg and make you wake up and listen. When all us kids would play out in the yard, she always kept an eye on us, and if she yelled at you, you *better* look up and see what she wanted! She was a good granny, and that's probably the reason we have turned out to be good ones, too."

Raymond and Bessie in later years

Rose Ella passed away in 1960,

and her old home was sadly deteriorating, so Raymond took it down in the early 1970s.

I asked if the family had electricity when they were growing up, and Barbara said, "In the mid-forties, I can still remember we used oil lamps; there was one in the middle of the kitchen table. But when the electric came through, everybody hooked onto it."

Peggy said, "Between Granny and Uncle Tommy and Aunt Ruth, it was more like having another set of parents. We were at their house a whole lot. They got the first television in the early 1950s, so we were always over there watching TV."

I asked what they thought of it, and Peggy said that they didn't have anything to compare it to, so they thought it was pretty wonderful. Barbara added, "The only thing we had to compare it to was the Victrola you had to wind up and play records on." When they were younger, they watched *Howdy Doody*; as teenagers, they watched *American Bandstand* with host Dick Clark.

Eventually, their family also got television and a telephone. Needing more space, Raymond tore out walls and added more rooms to the house.

The sisters as teenagers in identical dresses

Barbara laughed when she said, "Daddy would put on a porch, and it would turn into a room!" Peggy remembers at Barbara's sixteenth birthday party, the house was filled to overflowing with young people from the community.

Christmas was a happy time for the family. When asked if they'd had a tree, they said yes. Then Barbara looked at her sister and said, "How about that time we went down to cut a tree behind the Fields's place and Melvin Dodd's mule charged us?" I asked if they made it out, and both laughed and said, "We got the tree and just made it through the fence!" Both girls still have the doll-baby cradles that their parents got them one Christmas.

Peggy said, "Daddy worked hard to keep the family going. The first years, it was in apples, delivering them to Richmond for other people; farming; and then he got on at Basic Witz Furniture in Waynesboro. He worked there until the chemicals affected his sinuses, and then he had to leave. He did a little logging. He always took good care of us, and we always had something for Christmas. It wasn't a lot, but it wasn't important for it to be a whole lot. We heated the house with coal or wood, and it was always warm. We'd have meals with our families. We had hogs to butcher and a cow to milk. Thinking back, it was a good life!"

Barbara added, "We grew up on pinto beans, fried ham or shoulder, cornbread or hoecake. I remember a man by the name of Shafter "Shack" Brown, who lived on Glenthorne Loop, who would come and help Daddy butcher. Daddy would give him part of the meat for his help. He always wanted the chitlins', and Roger and I would go down to the creek and help him clean them, and they stunk so bad. I'd come in and Mama would have a fit because I would smell like the chitlins'. We had no idea what was in them, and after we found out, we wouldn't do them no more!"

For those of you who don't know what chitlins' are, they are the hog's intestines!

The Fitzgerald Sisters: Peggy Ballowe and Barbara Gormes 109

Peggy was the first in the family to marry and build a home across the road from her parents. Peggy met and courted James Ballowe for two years before being married on July 4, 1958, at the Bethlehem Church parsonage by Preacher Burkett.

Peggy and James on their wedding day with his mother, Pocahontas Johnston Ballowe (July 4, 1958)

James had a career in the navy for twenty-one years, the last six years spent in Washington, DC, as the executive officer for the presidential yacht *Sequoia*. Because James was gone so much, Peggy said that it was a good thing she was near her family. "We all looked after each other, took care of each other, and it was a comfort knowing you could look out the window at night to see the lights of your parents' or your brothers' and sisters' house."

After retirement, James started a home-improvement business that he and Peggy ran for more than thirty years. The Ballowes have three children: Wanda, Jimmy, and Lisa, who live close by; and two grandchildren, James Russell and Abigail, who are Jimmy's teenage children.

Barbara married Robert Lee "Buddy" Johnson on March 25, 1961, and moved to Georgia, where Buddy was stationed at Fort Benning. Their first child, Robert Lee, Jr. ("Bug"), was born in 1962. Rodney was born in 1965 while the couple was living in Delaware, as was Michelle, who was born in 1967. The marriage ended when Michelle was still a child. Barbara came back to live with her parents, finding employment first at Morton Frozen Foods and later at Basic Witz Furniture Factory.

James and Peggy today

She met her second husband, Billy Gormes, who had just come back from the service, at a dance/cookout at Van Riper's Lake in Greenfield. They married on November 13, 1971. The Gormeses built a house below Barbara's parents' place, where they continue to reside. Their daughter Jennifer was born in 1972, and she and her husband, Josh, now have a son, Brendan Joshua Scott, who is Barbara and Billy's only grandchild.

Billy and Barbara today

The Fitzgerald Sisters: Peggy Ballowe and Barbara Gormes

The four Fitzgerald siblings: Fuzzy, Barbara, Peggy, and Ray

Billy found work in the maintenance department at Wintergreen Ski Resort, and formally retired in 2011 after thirty-two years of service, although he still works there part time. Fuzzy and Ray built homes below that of their sisters, and three of their cousins, Roger, Dinky, and Toby, are just down the road. All of them own a piece of their grandfather Po Fitzgerald's original property.

Going back to Peggy's first reference to the '69 flood, I asked about the night of August 19, 1969, when Hurricane Camille ripped through Nelson County, Virginia, tearing the land in two.

Raymond and his brother Tommy lived along the South Fork of the Rockfish River that had been located on the opposite side of the road before the flood. Peggy and Barbara gave a harrowing account of that night, how it changed the landscape of their particular community and the devastation it caused.

Barbara said, "There was a lot of land over where Mama and Daddy lived. Their backyard used to be bigger than what it is today. Our uncle Tommy had a house, a huge garage, and some other big buildings to the left of Grandma's house, up on a hill. There were probably two or three acres with it, but the land went away when the river changed course, and the road was moved after the flood."

Peggy's husband, James, was still in the military, stationed in Washington, DC, at the time, and Peggy was home that night with their three children, Wanda, Jimmy, and Lisa. As Peggy tells it, "About ten o'clock, it was raining so hard we were on our knees looking out the window, and the kids were saying they wondered if it was raining frogs. We didn't think too much about it, because it had rained nearly every day that month.

"We went on to bed and about one o'clock in the morning, I heard this knock, and I got up and went to the door. It was my cousin Roger, who was coming home from working the night shift at Crompton plant in Waynesboro, and he told me to look in my front yard. I looked out, and water was about up to the flagpole, going down through the yard. He left and went home to his mama and daddy's house, and I went and got dressed and left the kids while I started walking across the road to Tommy's.

"The water was around my ankles, and Daddy and Ruth were out in the yard. I asked where Tommy was, and they said he was in the house, calling Barbara and some other people who worked at Morton Frozen Foods in Crozet, telling them not to come home. Tommy and Ruth's house sat on a hill with a lot of steps going up to it. I went in and said, 'Tommy, you all come over to my house, because if this thing gets bad, we can always go up in the mountains behind our house.' By the time I walked back home, the water had risen up to my knees and kept pushing me down.

"I finally made it to my front door and went in and got a huge umbrella and walked down to my brother Fuzzy's house and started beating on the door to get them up. I told them to come to my place, and he drove his logging truck up to let his wife, Jeanie, and their six-week-old baby, Nancy Jean, out before driving across the road to get Mama, Daddy, and Barbara's children. By this time the water was over the hood of the truck so he came back.

"In the meantime, Roger brought his mother and dad over to our house in a car but had gone back to get their cat and newborn kittens. He realized things were getting bad, so he and his brother, Toby, left the house and went over to be with Mama and Daddy. Several other neighbors who lived down the road called and asked if they could come, so we had a houseful. The river split right above Mama's house, coming down around it, but Tommy's house had a basement, and we figured the water came in and undermined it, and the house washed away.

Peggy's house the morning after the '69 flood

"About two o'clock in the morning, the road had turned into a river, and we watched all this debris coming down. Prior to this, we saw Ruth's car floating down through the yard. I had a flashlight and Mama had one, and we kept flashing them back and forth so we could see we were okay."

Fuzzy's house and damage from Camille

The torrential rain continued through the night, along with near-constant lightning that people said lit up the night sky like daylight. Barbara said that before she and some other employees who rode together to Morton's left for home after their shift, she heard her name called over the loudspeaker but never went back to see why they were calling her. If she had, she would have gotten the message left by her uncle Tommy to stay there.

Instead, the people carpooling together left Crozet and made it about halfway home before they witnessed a Volkswagen car ahead of them cross the flooded bridge over Goodwin's Creek and disappear into the water. They sat there until daylight, then made it as far as Route 6, where a lot of people were stranded because of high water. They continued on Route 151 and saw that the bridge over the Rockfish River had washed out, and the top part of a house along with the antennae was hanging off it.

They found out later that the couple who had lived in the house had washed away, and their bodies were found past the

Elk Hill Church on Route 664. Barbara said from that point they started to walk home; the road was completely gone, and there were people out everywhere, looking at the damage. They made it to Blanche Fields's home, which was heavily damaged, and the water was coming out of the mountains so swiftly that they could not cross it.

Lightning McGann laid a long ladder across a four-foot freshet of water, and one by one they crossed over on it. They picked their way up the mountain, and Barbara said that she stepped on something soft that gave way under her foot. When she looked down, she saw that it was one of Herman Fields's hogs. When they got up to Melba Fields's house, Barbara saw a bed and mattress standing up against a tree along with a chair and recognized them as her uncle Tommy's furniture.

She thought, "Oh, no, what are we going to find when we get home?" From there, they had to walk through the mountains to get the rest of the way home. The water was swift where they had to cross, and her companions made it across, but when Barbara started to wade through, some type of debris hit her and knocked her into the moving stream, and she thought she was done.

"If it hadn't been for Garth Fields, I know I would have drowned. Garth picked up a two-by-four and threw it to me, and it caught me in the ribs, pinning me up against a log truck until they could get to me."

When she finally made it home, the river was still running too high to cross to get to her parents and children. Barbara said that Bumpy Coffey will always be the love of her life, because he took his team of mules into the mountain and cut trees and hauled them out to make a wooden bridge over to her family. It was a joyous reunion, knowing everyone was safe, but in the end, there was much damage—the worst being that Tommy and Ruth's house was gone.

There was no electricity or phone service for weeks, and the sisters remember that their dad dragged an old King heater out into the yard and built a fire in it so that he could cook any food in the refrigerator that hadn't gone bad. Barbara said that after she had walked home, the leather penny loafers she had been wearing were completely eaten through, and the skin on her feet had peeled off from whatever was in the water.

Barbara said that there were places where the road had washed out in which you could put three tractor-trailers side by side. People were airlifted to the hospital in helicopters, and those remaining were left to salvage what was left of their belongings and begin the arduous task of cleanup. It was a long, slow recovery for the surviving people of Nelson County, Virginia, and the ravages of Camille can still be seen forty-six years later.

The extended Fitzgerald family (Christmas Eve 2011)

Today, the sisters keep busy with gardening, flowers, and yard sales, and they are both active members at the Mansfield's Piney Mountain Bible Camp. The large, extended Fitzgerald family remains close and sets a wonderful example for all families in the way they relate to one another. Every member is included at holiday get-togethers, and a packed house is the rule of thumb.

A special thank you goes out to all the Fitzgerald family members but especially Peggy and Barbara, who so willingly shared their memories of what life was like in the early years of the Beech Grove community.

Barbara and Peggy today

Irma Marshall Bowling Roberts

8

Irma Marshall Bowling Roberts

In giving a brief account of how I am acquainted with each person interviewed, I must admit that I've known Irma for years, but only through her daughter and son-in-law, Rosemary and Russell North. Each year, Russell sent in a renewal for Irma's *Backroads* subscription with the note: "For my ma-in-law." When I retired from the newspaper and went on to write books, Russell and Rosemary came to all my book signings; I began referring to them as my "groupies."

In the summer of 2013, the Norths came up for a visit; they brought Irma as well as Russell's mother with them, and I finally got to meet the "ma-in-law." A few weeks after Irma's one hundredth birthday, I asked Russell if Irma would consider letting me interview her for *Mountain Folk*, and to my delight, she accepted.

On October 2, 2014, Rosemary met me at the end of the road on which they all live, and I followed her up to her mother's house where the interview was to take place. It was a clear, cool fall day, and the farther up the mountain road we went, the better I liked it. The autumn colors were just starting to show. As we came to the end of the blacktop and started up a gravel lane with an "end state maintenance" sign, I began to smile.

My mother, bless her, used to visit from Florida, and I'd take her with me on some of my interviews for the newspaper. She would always say, "Lynn Anne, don't you know *anybody* that lives on a hard surfaced road?" I'd always reply, "Mom, if you want to talk to the mountain people, you have to go where they're at."

So riding up to Irma's was right down my alley, so to speak. When we came to her farm, I was surprised to see that she had no driveway; we had to park the vehicles at the bottom of the hill, open the wooden gate, and hoof it up to the house. Rosemary explained that her dad didn't want to have cars "driving over the hayfields."

As we entered the farmhouse, I looked around the old-fashioned kitchen with a big wood stove and felt right at home. It is a place filled with pictures of the family and a certain warmth that comes from years of happy living. Sorting through a box of the old black-and-white photos that accompany Irma's chapter, I was struck by how comfortable Rosemary and her mother made me feel. I think you'll feel it, too, as you read about this special lady and her amazing life.

Before I interviewed Irma, who celebrated her one hundredth birthday in 2014, her son-in-law, Russell, jotted down a few facts, putting her many years into perspective. The *Titanic* had sunk in 1912, two years prior to Irma's birth. The year she was born, Woodrow Wilson was president, World War I had just begun in Europe, and it had been fewer than a dozen years since the Wright brothers had made their historic flight in Kitty Hawk, North Carolina, in 1903.

We all live through a certain slice of history, but it's an amazing experience to talk to a person who can remember what life was like nearly a hundred years before the basics of modern-day living were even available. Irma not only remembers but willingly shares her memories with anyone having an ear to listen.

Irma was born in Arrington, Virginia, and said that the village was always small. It consisted of a country store run by Bud Farrar, a post office where Irma remembers Mr. Foster was the postmaster, a railway station where Mr. Strother was the station agent, and a large cold-storage building where apple growers from all over the county brought their fruit to store for the winter. Irma said that her family lived in a two-story frame house about a mile and a half from the village, in the "suburbs" of Arrington, near the Centenary Methodist Church.

Irma's parents were John Waller Bowling and Sadie Irene Thacker Bowling. They had known each other all their lives and married in 1907. Before marriage, Irma's father had been a carpenter for the railroad, building bridges and anything else the railway needed. After he married Sadie, he became a full-time farmer.

John's parents were David Waller Bowling and Pettis Maria Loving Bowling. When Irma's parents got married, John's father bought them a small farm and built the couple a house to start out with. He did this for two of his four children; the other two already had places of their own.

Irma's parents,
John and Sadie Bowling (1908)

Sadie's parents were George Watson Thacker and Rebecca Marguerite Humphries Thacker. Both sets of grandparents farmed for a living.

John and Sadie began their family a year after they married and had three children: Waller Duval, born in 1908; Irma

The Arrington house where Irma grew up

Marshall, born on September 13, 1914; and the youngest, John Alvin, born in 1918. Irma said that her older brother, Duval, was thought to have been oxygen deprived at birth and "never matured as he should have."

I asked Irma what she remembered about growing up almost a hundred years ago, and I casually mentioned that I guessed she had to help with all the farm chores. I got a big surprise when Irma laughed and replied, "No, I never did!" When asked how she got out of doing farm work, Rosemary volunteered that her mother, as the only girl, might have been somewhat spoiled. "Why, she wouldn't even eat her green beans unless her daddy stacked them up in the shape of a little square box."

Irma added, "I was right spoiled. I never even learned to cook until after I was married." Although the family kept a garden and the typical farm animals—a milk cow, chickens, hogs, and a horse—Irma said that she never helped take care of them, preferring to work indoors, helping her mother with the housework. She learned how to embroider and made quite a few scarves and pillowcases as she was growing up.

Christmas at the Bowlings featured a big dinner that Sadie cooked and visits with the family. A tree was cut and decorated in the home with paper ornaments, and Irma said that they hung stockings up on Christmas Eve that "Santa" would fill with candy, oranges, nuts, and perhaps a toy. Irma said, "I was a firm believer in Santa Claus until an older child told me he wasn't real." There was a special holiday program at their church and in school, and Irma remembers reciting poetry at both events.

Irma has always loved to read and explained, "I had a friend who was ahead of me in school, and her mother was a teacher. Her mother taught her how to read, and the girl took it on herself to teach me before I started first grade."

Irma walked to the Arrington School, which was about a mile

The old Arrington School (c. 1930)

and a half away from her home. The school went up to the seventh grade, and Irma remembers that her cousin's wife, Mrs. Leonard Bowling, was her first-grade teacher; Miss Coakley and Mrs. Massie Yuille were two other teachers. After completing all grades at Arrington, Irma rode a bus to the early Lovingston High School, a two-story building that had fallen into such disrepair, the structure was anchored to the ground to keep it from falling over.

This was before Route 29 was constructed, so the road from Arrington to the high school wound around Diggs' Mountain, past the mansion at Oak Ridge, through Shipman, and up Route 56 to Lovingston. Back then, the high schools consisted of freshman, sophomore, junior, and senior years (grades nine through twelve). It wasn't until sometime in the 1960s that an eighth grade was added to the school program. A new brick high school was built (the current Nelson Center), and that's where Irma began her senior year in the fall of 1931.

The students graduated early in April of the following year, because the county didn't have enough money for the school's operating expenses. Irma was one of thirteen seniors graduating in 1932; their ceremony was held inside the Lovingston movie theater. She is the last surviving member of the class of 1932.

Irma as a young woman at Crabtree Falls (1931)

When asked if her parents had a vehicle, Irma said that neither her mother nor her father ever learned to drive, so they had no use for a car or truck. She

Girls of the class of 1932; Irma is kneeling at left

remembers riding with her father in a horse-drawn wagon to Variety Mills, where they took wheat and corn to be ground into flour and meal that the family consumed. To this day, Irma, like her parents, does not drive. She confided that she actually did learn and went to take the driving test, but the instructor said that she was too nervous and wouldn't let her take it, so she never pursued it any further.

After she graduated school, Irma had a hard time finding employment, so for the next eight years, she remained at home. These were the years of the Great Depression, and jobs were hard to come by. In 1940, Irma's aunt told her that she knew some girls who had found work at Sweet Briar College, waiting on the privileged girls who were students there.

"My brother took me for an interview one day, and I had to come back the next day to find out if I got the job." Irma said that she was hired, and one of her duties was to put linen tablecloths and napkins on the dining tables for each meal, along with place settings of china that had the Sweet Briar emblem on them and real silver tableware. When the students were done eating, Irma was to clear the tables and clean up. If a girl was sick or just wanted to stay in her room, the hired help had to take a tray with the meal up to them.

Irma sometimes helped out with preparing the salad bar, and one of the jobs was to take the seeds out of grapes. Irma said, "Oh, we hated that job!" For her work, Irma received free room, board, and meals, along with twenty-one dollars a month. Of her paycheck, Irma said, "I thought I was rich!" She said that there were also student waitresses; girls working their way through college by doing the same work that Irma did.

I asked what the well-to-do students studied and what types of degrees they were interested in. I had a good laugh when I was told, "They were working towards their MRS degree." When pressed further, I was informed the letters stood for "Mrs." In other words, many of the girls were simply going to college in the hopes of finding a husband. Irma worked at her Sweet Briar job for two years.

She then found work in the lab at the American Cyanamid Company in Piney River. Irma had a girlfriend who worked there who helped Irma get a job. At this time, these jobs were available for young women because so many men went into the military.

The plant made titanium dioxide, which was used, among other things, as a coating for refrigerators and stoves

Irma at Sweet Briar College (1942)

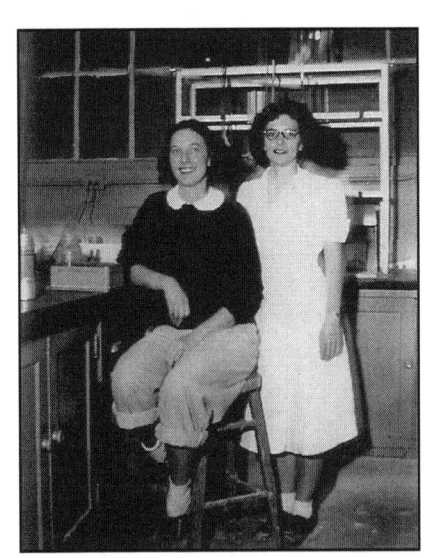

Irma (left) at the American Cyanamid lab (mid-1940s)

and in high-grade automobile paint. The process took many stages of development, and, in the lab, Irma had to test each stage before the process was complete. She said that one of the funniest things that happened to her at that time took place at the Canody boarding house in Piney River, where she was staying.

She and her girlfriend shared a room and a bed, and her friend kept getting bitten at night while they slept. They

The American Cyanamid plant in Piney River (mid-1940s)

turned the mattress over and found an infestation of bed bugs. Irma said, "I had never seen them before and didn't know what they were. They didn't bite me. They don't bite some people. We drug the mattress and bed frame outside and poured boiling water on the frame, and we didn't have any more after that. The lady who owned the boarding house claimed she didn't know about the bed bugs, but every once in a while we'd smell kerosene." Kerosene was often used to spray for these types of pests.

Another funny thing happened at the boarding house. One night, Irma and her roommate were sleeping and awoke to a strange man opening the door and looking in at them. Irma went to Mr. Canody and told him what had happened. He got his gun and began searching all the rooms for the intruder. He was found in another room and everyone had a laugh when it was discovered that the "intruder" was Mr. Canody's nephew, who had come in unannounced and was just trying to go to bed in his old room, the one the girls were now occupying.

Irma worked five days a week on a mixed-shift schedule, so on her days off, she would go home to Arrington. Rosemary confessed that after her mother had started working and begun to date, she had a lot of boyfriends. Several of these men asked Irma to marry them, but she always said no; she didn't want

Irma with her mother, Sadie (1942)

to get married, she was having too much fun.

Irma loved to travel, and saved her money to buy train tickets to places like New York City and upstate New York as far as the Canadian border. She traveled with her girlfriend, Julia Warner. Irma remembers going to the top of the Empire State Building plus seeing all the other sights the city had to offer during her one-week stay.

It was on this trip to New York that Irma saw her first television in a store window. A person at the store asked the girls where they were from and filmed while they talked; then he instantly showed them on the television screen. When asked what she thought about being on TV, Irma said, "Well, I thought it was pretty neat, I guess."

The Bowling family: (left to right) Rebecca Scott, Nettie Loving, Irma, Mary Lee Bowling, John Alvin, and Sadie

Another time, she and her cousin took a train to Detroit, Michigan, where her cousin was reunited with her husband. Irma traveled to Jamestown and Virginia Beach quite a few times and many places in between.

Irma had met her future husband, Nelson William Roberts, in high school. Nelson was two years older than Irma, born on March 13, 1912. His family lived on Old Roberts Mountain Road in Faber and to get to school, he rode his horse up the long dirt road to Route 6. There he corralled the animal at someone's house and caught the bus to Lovingston High School. When the school day was over, he'd take the bus back to where his horse was and ride it on home.

Irma Marshall Bowling (1946)

Irma said that after they'd both graduated, he came to see her one time while she was still living at home. "I was surprised when he came, but after he left, twelve years went by, and I didn't see him anymore. At the end of the twelve years, he came back."

When asked what they would do on a typical date, Irma said that they would go bowling or to the movies in Lynchburg. She and Nelson courted

Nelson William Roberts as a young man (1936)

for about five years before marrying on January 21, 1951. The couple eloped to North Carolina, and they were married by a preacher in the church parsonage. They took a week-long honeymoon to Daytona Beach, Florida.

I asked why they hadn't gotten married closer to home, and Irma made me laugh by saying, "I didn't want to! Everyone was always asking, 'When are you going to get married? When are you going to get married?' I was thirty-six years old, and I didn't want to tell anybody when I was getting married."

When the newlyweds came back to Nelson County, Irma continued to work at the Piney River plant for another two years, staying with her parents in Arrington while Nelson was in the process of fixing up an old tenant house on his family property. Nelson was a farmer, so Irma finally learned how to cook and become a farm wife to her new husband. They formally moved into the renovated home sometime in 1953, and Irma traded her lab coat for an apron, becoming a full-time housewife.

Nelson and Irma before they married

Nelson's grandfather, Henry Harris Roberts, owned a very large tract of land along Hickory Creek, and he gave each of his five children a piece of the property to farm when they were older. Nelson's father was Milton Steptoe Roberts, and his mother was Sarah Harris Roberts. Milton and Sarah were given the section of land called "Mountain View" on Old Roberts Mountain Road, where Nelson grew up.

Irma and Nelson had not been married long when her daddy died suddenly at sixty-seven years of age. He had gone to bed and asked his wife to please bring him a drink of water when she came to bed. By the time she was ready to turn in and brought the glass of water, he had died, probably from a heart attack. Sadie and her son Duval continued to live together, and in the mid-1960s, they moved from Arrington to Massies Mill.

Hurricane Camille hit Nelson County on the night of August 19, 1969, and the flood waters picked up Sadie's house and wedged it in between a tree and another structure. Had that not happened, they would have washed away. They rode out the harrowing storm, and the next day, they were taken to the Lynchburg Hospital to be checked over.

After that time, Duval went to live at the Central Virginia Training Center in Lynchburg. Irma's mother stayed with relatives for a time. When a new trailer was obtained and set next to the Robertses' home, Sadie lived there until 1974. That same summer, Sadie suffered a series of debilitating strokes and was moved to a nursing facility, where she passed away in 1978.

Five years into the marriage, at forty-one years of age, Irma had her first child: a daughter they named Rosemary Nelson Roberts, born on February 2, 1956. Their second and last child was a son: David Garland Roberts, who was born on July 1, 1958.

In addition to farming, Nelson was also the rural route mail carrier for Faber. At that time,

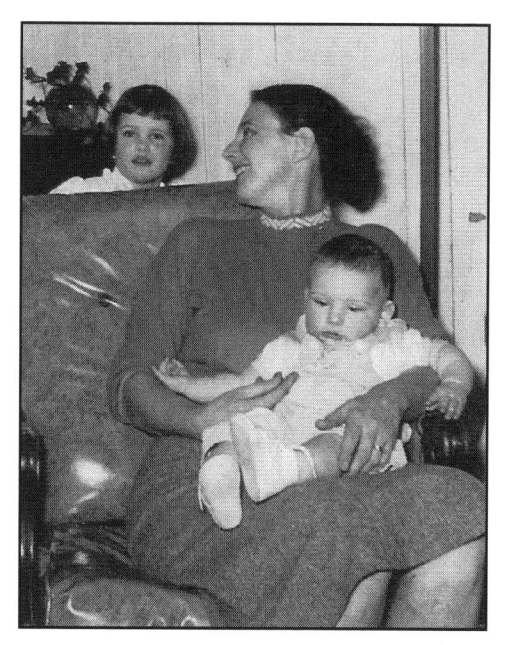

Irma with her two children, Rosemary and David (1959)

the route encompassed the village of Faber, down "Sidetrack" (which was a strip behind the Faber post office), down Route 29, and across Adial to the Nellysford post office, where he would drop off a bag of mail. He then went up all the mountain hollows, such as Stoney Creek and Spruce Creek, Berry Hill Lane, Duncan Hollow Loop, and other surrounding areas.

Rosemary said that her dad would leave the house at seven in the morning and come home at two o'clock in the afternoon. "He got off the mail route at two o'clock and got on a tractor and farmed until dark. He had this job from 1962 until 1982 and wore one car out every year because of the bad roads."

The Roberts had an apple orchard, peach trees, and other fruit trees. Nelson made hay for his cows, and Irma had a large garden across Hickory Creek, and she had to cross a little bridge to get to it. She canned all the fruits and vegetables that were raised on their 115 acres.

Rosemary said that when she was growing up, the Hickory Creek area was filled with apple orchards owned by members of the Quick, Roberts, Bradshaw, and Davidson families. Rosemary said that they know early Indians inhabited the land at one time because of the abundance of arrowheads her daddy

Nelson in later years on the farm (late 1980s)

plowed up with his tractor. There is still a flat rock on the property that was probably used as a grinding stone.

Up to very recently, Irma enjoyed knitting, crocheting, crossword puzzles, reading, and taking care of her flowers, for which she had an exceptional green thumb. But at a hundred years of age, her eyes aren't as good as they once were. She was also an excellent seamstress, and sewed all her own clothes as well as her daughter's, from the time Rosemary was in the fifth grade through her college years.

On Irma's milestone birthday in 2014, there was a family party, and she received 112 birthday congratulatory cards from friends and members of her family. She is still a great cook, and Rosemary showed me a picture of a beautiful lat-

Irma on the front porch of her home (September 2, 2001)

ticework apple pie that Irma had made for Rosemary's husband's birthday. Rosemary and Russell North live down the road from Irma, and Irma's son David lives just across the hill, so if she needs anything, they can be reached quickly. In addition to her two children, Irma has three grandchildren: Jeremy Roberts and Richard and Rosanne North. She also has two great-grandchildren: Logan and Caroline Roberts.

Rosemary is the Clerk of the General District Court and works in Lovingston, and Russell retired five years ago from the Central Virginia Electrical Co-op. David is self-employed and has a roofing business.

Nelson passed away in 1993 from leukemia. The family thinks it was caused by all the sprays he used in treating the apple trees over the years. Irma continues to live in the same white house she's called home for more than sixty years.

Irma's grandfather, George Thacker, fought in the Civil War. His spunky wife, Rebecca, rode a horse from Montebello to Scottsville and boarded a packet boat going down the Kanawha Canal, so that she could visit her husband who was fighting at the Battle of Seven Pines. I told Irma that I could certainly see where she got her plucky and adventuresome spirit!

Irma and her grandchildren, Jeremy Roberts and Rosanne and Richard North (2006)

We wound up the interview with much laughter as Rosemary served us sweet tea and lemon, along with generous slices of lemon chiffon pie. Before I left, I took photographs of Irma and Rosemary, as well as the farm outbuildings with their backdrop of surrounding mountains. What a beautiful place. What wonderful people. What a perfect afternoon.

Irma and her daughter, Rosemary (October 2, 2014)

Martin Samuel "Buddy" Truslow

9

Martin Samuel "Buddy" Truslow

I met Buddy and Gracie Truslow in February 2005, at the one hundredth birthday party for Gracie's mother, Lizzie Wood, that was held at the Waynesboro Church of the Brethren. Gracie said that it was the first formal party her mother had ever had and that she was thrilled. I remember asking Gracie where her mother was, thinking I was looking for a frail little woman, perhaps on a walker. When Gracie pointed to a pert little lady, dressed in a pink suit, who was busy visiting with all her guests, I knew this was a special family. I felt honored to have been asked to cover the party and write an article about it for *Backroads* newspaper.

From that time on, we have been friends. In February 2014, I made a trip to Lizzie's home to celebrate her 109th (yes, you read that correctly) birthday and to write a story about this amazing woman for the *Staunton News Leader*. The last thing Lizzie said to me that day was, "You *will* be at my 110th birthday, won't you?" I told Lizzie that I wouldn't miss it for the world!

When the idea came to write this new book, I knew I wanted to interview Lizzie's son-in-law, Buddy Truslow, who had grown up the old way on Stoney Creek. We met at their home in Waynesboro and had a delightful morning talking about his early years. It was there that Gracie told me that the first time she met my husband, Billy, and his family, they were singing bluegrass gospel music at the Waynesboro Mennonite Church. What a happy coincidence that she would have met my future husband before we were married, then invite both of us to Lizzie's birthday party all those years later.

So in a roundabout way, our association has come full circle, as I've interviewed both Lizzie and her daughter's husband, Buddy. I hope you all enjoy his story as much as I did.

⁂

Martin Samuel Truslow came into the world on February 27, 1931, the fifth of six children born to Wilmont Rondue "Ballie" Truslow and Melinda Myrtle Puckett Truslow, who lived in Nelson County, Virginia, close to the little village of Nellysford. Nellie Cook was the midwife who delivered him, and although he doesn't know where the nickname "Buddy" came from, it has been with him his whole life.

His siblings, by order of their birth, were: Alice, Annie, Mary, Herbert, and Yvonne. At the time of his birth, the family was on a farm simply known as the "Allen place." At some point while they were still living there, Ballie, in addition to farming, was employed by the Highway Department (VDOT) for about fif-

Paternal grandparents, Jefferson and Alice Truslow (August 27, 1920)

teen years. The Trulsows' two closest neighbors at that time were the Napiers and the midwife who delivered Buddy, Nellie Cook.

Buddy's grandparents on his father's side were Jefferson Napoleon Truslow and Alice Dameron Truslow. His maternal grandparents were Walter Puckett and Susan Margaret Thompson Puckett.

Around 1935, before Buddy started school, the Truslows moved from the Allen place to the mountain side of Stoney Creek. A large tract of land owned by the government, known as "The Big Survey," covered a large portion of the mountains. Buddy remembers men cutting extract wood off the land, and, for each cord they brought out, they had to pay a fee to Mr. Dall Small, who lived at the foot of

Maternal grandparents, Susan and Walter Puckett with Elder J. F. Broadhead (August 25, 1920)

Buddy's paternal grandparents and their two sons, W. R. "Ballie" and Vernon

the mountain. He, in turn, would collect the money and turn it over to the owner. Extract wood was dead standing chestnut trees, referred to as "stumpage," that had been killed by blight.

The family lived on the mountain top farm at the head of Stoney Creek until 1951, then they moved farther down the creek, closer to the main road.

"I was glad to get off the mountain," Buddy said. "I like mountains, but when you live back that far, you don't see nobody. By that time, my older sister Alice married and moved next to the creek, but that was about three-quarters of a mile away from where we lived. Cashus and Lillie Napier would always visit, and we had a path around through the mountain to our houses."

Buddy's parents on the front porch of their home on Stoney Creek

The government land was bought by a William Maddox of North Carolina around 1952. Twenty years later, in the early 1970s, the land was ultimately bought by Cabot, Cabot, and Forbes, the company responsible for building Wintergreen Ski Resort on land once described as having no recreational value.

The property to which the Truslows moved was located just below where Mr. "Pal" Thompson lived and had a small store. Some of the original families living up and down Stoney Creek were the Davises, Thompsons, McGanns, Truslows, and Campbells. Buddy said that back then, there were probably seventy or eighty people living in that particular hollow, and "they were all good people.

In recalling the various stores that operated in the area, Buddy said that when the family still lived back at the Allen place, they went to Forrest Hughes's store, which was located in Nellysford at Route 151, right next to Forrest's house. "We would walk down and cut across Graveyard Hill and down to the store."

Buddy said that they operated on the no-money-exchanged policy; if a person brought in fresh eggs or butter to trade, Forrest would give them a "due bill." This was a handwritten IOU credit slip that could be applied to anything bought at the store.

Forrest Hughes's store; his daughter Suzie is the one in the foreground

Buddy said that his father's brother, Jesse Truslow, was a blacksmith who had a shop close to Forrest Hughes's store. There was also another store to the rear of Forrest Hughes's house, closer to Adial Road, that was run by a Mr. Dodd.

In the 1940s, Mulford Campbell built a store on Route 151 close to Stoney Creek Road, but it burned down. He later rebuilt and ran it for a time. After that, Les Graves owned and operated the store, changing its name to Graves Grocery. It is still called Graves today, although it is no longer owned by that family.

Pal Thompson also had a store up on Stoney Creek. He would sit on the porch of his house until a customer came to buy something, then he'd walk over to wait on them. Buddy said, "In the wintertime, you had to knock on Mr. Thompson's door and tell him you needed something, and he'd open the store and get you what you wanted." Much later, Buddy's family bought Mr. Thompson's property, and Buddy's daddy, weather permitting, would sit on the porch waiting for customers, just like Mr. Thompson had.

Grover Harris had a store and a large gristmill at the foot of Spruce Creek, and Buddy remembers that his dad would put him on the horse with a big sack of corn and send him down to get it ground. "Daddy would tell me, 'You go down to Grover, and if he already has some ground, he'll just trade you, and you come back with that. If he don't, he'll grind your corn and put it back on the horse for you.' And back up the mountain I would go."

Mr. Pal Thompson's store

Buddy remembers when the property where Lake Monacan is now was nothing but a large flat where his daddy raised sugar cane to make sorghum molasses in the fall. When the lake was first dug, it was part of a Boy Scout camp; then when the land was bought for the Stoney Creek housing development, they renamed it Lake Monacan.

The Truslows always had a big garden, and Buddy said that his daddy had horses, but he also had a plow mule. "A mule is the best thing for a garden. They have small feet to get in between the rows and take things a little slower than a horse. He kept the mule until he got so he couldn't work the garden, then he let my Uncle Vernon have him."

Vernon Truslow was Ballie's brother, and he lived up on Spruce Creek. When *Backroads* newspaper started, Vernon and his wife, Clora, were a couple of my first interviews. Buddy's wife, Gracie, and I compared notes about the way the water in Vernon and Clora's kitchen sink had run continuously, because it was gravity-fed from the spring.

Buddy said, "When I was young, I used to love to go up to Uncle Vernon's. My cousins, Wesley, Carol, and Jack, were there, so Mother would write a note to Aunt Clorie and give it to someone who would deliver it to her, and she'd write a note back saying it was okay for me to get off the bus and come spend the night with them. Mama would write, 'Well, you'll have to feed him and pack his lunch.'"

Buddy started school in Nellysford, where there were two buildings: one for the elementary classes and another for high school. The principal was Mr. J. D. Lawman at the time, and when recess was over, he'd come out on the porch and ring a bell to bring the children back to class. Buddy attended this early school for just a few years before the new Rockfish School was completed in 1939, and students had to ride a bus for the five-mile distance. Up to that time, everyone walked to school, to church, and everywhere else, since they didn't have vehicles.

To show how times have changed, Buddy told me that all the kids were brought to the new school before the new term began to show them how to use an indoor bathroom. The Nellysford School still had outdoor privies, at that time—one for the girls and one for the boys—so most of the children had never seen the likes of an indoor bathroom. Buddy laughed and said that when they first lived up in the mountains, "We didn't even have an outdoor toilet; we just went in the bushes."

The Rockfish School had eleven grades. Grade school consisted of classes one through seven, and high school had four years, grades eight, nine, ten, and eleven. When asked about how discipline within the school system had changed over the years, Buddy said, "You didn't do too much; you didn't do too much wrong back then. One teacher had a habit of slapping you on the hand if you did something wrong, either with a ruler or with her hand." But Buddy was a well-behaved boy and can't remember ever being punished.

Buddy at twelve years of age *Gracie at twelve years of age*

The Truslow family always attended the Wintergreen Christian Church, located at the base of Spruce Creek Road, and they walked from Stoney Creek each Sunday to attend services. Buddy recalls that there was a large wood stove in the center of the one-room church that had a flue pipe going straight up through the roof. In the summer months, the stove would be taken out, along with the flue pipe, to make more room for the congregation.

During the winter, Buddy and his friend, Steve Thompson, would walk over early in the morning to start a fire in the stove so that it would be warm when the people came. The children had Sunday school before the eleven o'clock service began. A yearly homecoming service was held in the summer, along with a two-week revival. Baptisms were done in the "Buck Hole," which Buddy said was their playhouse.

"There was a big rock, ten or twelve feet wide, that sat against the bank that people could sit on. In the springtime, the adults would clean up the brush from around the edge and dam up the water with rocks to baptize in and also to let the children swim in. It was about six feet at the deep end, about three feet at the small end, so the little children could play in it. That was the meetin' place after church. Us kids would swim while the older people watched from the rock."

Buddy's first car was a 1940 Chevrolet; the first one, he said, that had enough power to get up the mountain! Back then, the roads were dirt but solid. I asked where he got the money to buy a car at seventeen or eighteen years of age. He said that when he was younger, he did odd jobs for Bosby Small and Dick Truslow, and he also drove a dump truck, hauling rock from the Rockfish River to the crushing machine, when they were repaving Route 151.

One day, Buddy came home from work, and there was a letter waiting for him from Uncle Sam, saying he would be drafted into the military (marines) in March 1951, just a few weeks after his twentieth birthday. He went to basic training at Parris Island, South Carolina, which was a real eye-opener for a mountain boy.

Eighteen-year-old Buddy with his horse

"I hadn't been nowhere. I didn't know nothing or how other people talked. Why, I was twelve years old before I ever went to Waynesboro!"

After basic training, he came home for ten days, then was sent to Camp Lejeune, North Carolina, and put in the mess hall, doing everything from peeling potatoes to serving up food. "After a few weeks, they came and told me to pack up all my belongings, because that night I was to catch a train and go to Florida to be part of an abandoned navy base near Miami, where we were supposed to make it into the 3rd Marine Air Wing."

Buddy explained that he was a "crash crewman" for the Marine Corp Air Station. A crash crewman was basically the same thing as a modern-day firefighter, except they fought fires on airplanes that had been sent out on training missions and maybe caught fire while landing. Back then, they were all prop planes; only one jet was used as a trainer.

"I was there for about a year when this old colonel came in with a bunch of papers in his hand and said, 'Here's your orders. You will leave today, and we'll give you three days to get to Cherry Point, North Carolina, to report in. You will then get on a boat for duty "beyond the seas."' That means you are going overseas to fight. So I went to Cherry Point, where they told us we were going to Norfolk, Virginia, where I got on a ship. We left Norfolk and stopped at Port Everglades, Florida, to pick up more troops. We got out on open water, and we were the flagship for four other ships.

"We wound up in the Panama Canal, which is really something to see work. We left there and went to San Diego, California. The next day, we left, but they wouldn't tell us where we were going. Seven days later, they told us we were going to Yokohama, Japan. When we got to Yokohama, we had been on the water thirty-eight days and traveled 12,500 some miles and never got off.

"I stayed on the firefighting crew the whole time I was over there. When it was time to come home, they put me on what they called a flying boxcar to someplace in Japan. Seven days later, we boarded a troop transport ship bound for San Diego.

Buddy as a marine (1953)

On the way back, we hit a bad storm, and the front end of the ship would go completely under the water. I was discharged in San Diego and came home in 1953."

Buddy said that he went all the way to Japan and never got hurt, but as a child, he came close to getting killed twice. When he was four or five years old, he climbed up on the barn manger where the horses ate. He was looking to get a piece of baling twine for something, but one of the horses reached up and grabbed onto his chest and pulled him down into the manger.

Buddy said, "I don't know how I got out of there, but I come out of there! I never said nothing about it to my parents, but my mother must have been giving me a bath or getting me dressed and saw the bruise, and I never went to the barn no more!"

The other time he had a close call was when he was staying with his sister Alice and her family, and the house caught on fire after they had gone to bed. "It was early in the morning, and someone grabbed me and shook me and told me to get up, the house was on fire. So I jumped up and grabbed my britches at the end of the bed, but the ceiling had fallen down and was melting all over us. We ran out and jumped off the porch and didn't get hurt, but the whole house burned down."

I asked if it had been hard adjusting to being back on Stoney Creek after traveling around the world in the marines. Buddy said, "It was a long run, but I wouldn't take anything in the world for it. I've seen things and done things I never dreamed of. I would never have believed I'd a woke up in Japan."

Buddy was twenty-two years old when he returned and began dating girls. Gracie Wood was one of them. She was born in Earlysville on April 13, 1931, the fourth child of nine born to Rubin and Lizzie Wood, who were living in Fishersville at the time. She was supposed to marry a boy who was in the navy, but in the meantime Buddy had come home, and, by chance, she went out on a date with him.

They became friends, but it was understood that Gracie would be marrying the other fellow when he got out of the navy. In her words, "But after a while, Buddy asked me to reconsider marrying the other boy, and one night we pulled off on the Parkway, and he told me to open the [glove compartment] in the car. There was a bag in there, and he told me to take it out, and I saw it was a little ring box, and that's when he gave me my diamond."

At that time, all the young people met up at a place called Donut Dinette in Waynesboro. Many of their friends were there, and after Buddy had given Gracie the ring, they went in to show it off. The boy she had originally planned to marry came home and begged her to break it off with Buddy, but Gracie told him no, she couldn't do that, because she was in love with him.

Buddy worked at DuPont two or three different times, but kept getting laid off, so they postponed their wedding. Gracie was working at the White Brother's department store in Waynesboro, where she started out as a salesperson. She then became the buyer for piece-goods and notions and the store's window dresser.

Buddy did not have a steady job but was helping Gracie's father on the farm when they decided to go ahead and get married. On Thursday night, October 20, 1955, the young couple tied the knot at Wintergreen Christian Church. Rev. Elwood Campbell and just a few of their family members were in attendance. Gracie laughs at the remembrance of Elwood having forgotten that he had scheduled a young people's meeting on the same night and having to tell the children to sit quietly in the back of the church until he could marry the Truslows.

Gracie said, "When we came out to get in the car, those young people had tied tin cans to the bumper and put signs on the back of the car. Buddy took them off before we drove to Charlottesville to see his brother Herbert and his wife, Polly. When we left their house and were driving through Richmond, each time we would stop at a light, people would drive up to the car yelling, 'You'll be *sorry!*' Buddy missed one of the signs the kids had put on the car. We drove to Williamsburg where we spent the night."

The newlyweds came back to an apartment in Waynesboro that they had previously furnished, and set up housekeeping. Buddy found work at Brand Chevrolet, washing and delivering cars. He did that for several years before filling out an application and being hired by the Dawbarn Corporation in 1959. This company changed names several times, but most people knew it by Wayne-Tex in later years. Buddy worked there for thirty-three years and nine months as a machine operator before retiring in 1993.

The Truslows' first Christmas (1955)

Gracie had a similar experience when White Brother's Department Store became White's Incorporated then later the Southern Department Store, where she was the assistant manager. She retired from Southern in 1978 but was bored at home, so she took a job with First and Merchants Bank, first as a teller and later as the safety deposit clerk. She then moved to the bookkeeping department and did a few other types of jobs before permanently retiring in 1991.

They had moved from their first apartment to one on Sherwood Avenue, then to another on DuPont Boulevard. They bought their first house on Florence Avenue in Waynesboro and finally settled where they are now on Belvue.

Back on Stoney Creek, Buddy ended up buying the two houses and the property that his parents had owned and fixed up one of the homes to use as a weekend getaway. In later years, the Truslows sold both places to Jim and Twilla Jean Truslow, who live across the road from the properties on Stoney Creek.

Buddy and Gracie's twenty-fifth anniversary

Today, Buddy and Gracie lead active lives and enjoy going to auctions, looking for collectables. Although they were never blessed with children, the Truslows claim David Showers as their own. David and his family were members of Gracie's family, and he spent a lot of time with Buddy and Gracie while growing up and as an adult, and he still visits regularly.

The Truslows now attend Mount Vernon Church of the Brethren, which is much closer to them, and Gracie often stays with her sweet mother when her brother Maynard, who lives with Lizzie, leaves on a trip.

Lizzie is now more than 109 years of age and continues to live in her own home, doing a bit of cooking and the laundry,

Gracie and her mother, Lizzie Wood

and still winning at the board games she likes to play in the evenings after supper. At this writing, Lizzie's nine children still survive, and the photo below shows six generations of the same family. From left to right, they are: Lizzie G. Wood; her daughter Thelma Bryant; and Thelma's multi-generational family, Stanley, Cara, Caitlyn, and Peyton Bryant.

Six generations of the Wood family

As the interview came to a close, we all walked out into the Truslows' spacious backyard that borders a beautiful wood, and it was under the trees where the photos of Buddy and Gracie were taken. They still make a handsome couple, and in October 2015, the Truslows will celebrate their sixtieth wedding anniversary. So many memories, such a happy life together. May God continue to bless you both in the years ahead, and my special thanks go out to each of you for being a part of *Mountain Folk*.

Buddy and Gracie Truslow (2014)

Maybelle Campbell, Montebello, Virginia

Betty Marie Bryant Roberts

10

Betty Marie Bryant Roberts

It's hard to say when I first bumped into Betty, her husband, Lester, and their family. I probably met Lester before Betty because of my early association with the Blue Ridge Parkway where he worked for so many years. But then, as I frequented Montebello, gathering stories for *Backroads* newspaper, I met Betty's mother, Lois Bryant, at various senior functions held at the Montebello Store and Fire Department. One thing's for sure, when my husband became the pastor of Mount Paran Baptist Church in Montebello, we got to know their whole family intimately and watched the "little kids" mature into "big kids" with kids of their own.

Betty is full of life, and her humorous stories down through the years have always tickled me. I knew I wanted her to be part of *Mountain Folk* the minute I decided to write it, and she tickled me even more by saying she'd do it! Let me introduce you to Betty Roberts as she gives her upbeat opinion of the ups and downs of life, as only she can.

❦

Betty's maternal grandparents were Cornealius Washington Bradley and Beulah Roberta Campbell Bradley. At the time, the Bradleys were living in the mountain community of Coffeytown in one of the abandoned shanties that had been built along the Dinky Railroad line that ran through the mountains, hauling logs to the sawmill in Cornwall. The Bradleys had six children: Lloyd, Ezra, Wilber, Lois Helen (born November 23, 1914), Florine, and Madge.

The log house that Beulah lived in after her husband died

In May 1930, Cornealius died at age thirty-seven of tuberculosis, leaving his wife to care for their family. Beulah moved to Montebello and took up residence in a small log house located on Fork Mountain. Later, she lived in two subsequent homes on the same property. Betty said that her Grandma Beulah always slept with a small pistol under her pillow.

Beulah later married Frank Phillips and had two more children, Delbert and Maxine. Beulah's oldest daughter, Lois, married Melvin Zirkle Bryant, and the young couple moved down the mountain to what they called the "lower place," where Beulah had lived years before. There was also a house up the road, called the "upper place," where they lived until their son Bobby was born.

The two-story weatherboard house on Fork Mountain

The family then moved into an older, two-story weatherboard home on the Bryant property, where Betty was born on August 16, 1948, the eighth child of ten.

Lois and Melvin's children, by order of birth, were: Christine, who was born in January 1933 but died a month later; Glennwood, in 1934; Edgar, in 1936; Wendell, in 1939; Milton, in 1941; Frances, in 1944; Bobby, in 1946; Betty, in 1948; Gorman, in 1949; and Phyllis, in 1954.

Betty said that one of the midwives who helped her mother deliver her babies was Bessie Phillips. Betty said that her mother had a hard labor with Edgar, because he was so big. "Mama said Bessie stood at the end of the bed began to pray, 'Lord, it's all in your hands; I've done all I can do for her.' Mama thought, 'Oh, Lord, I'm going to die.' But Edgar finally came and weighed ten pounds at birth."

Betty's grandparents on her father's side were William Franklin Bryant and Annette L. Ramsey Bryant, who were both born in 1884 and died in the 1960s. The Bryants also had six children: Melvin, who was born on February 2, 1908; David; Russell; Walton; Fishburn; and baby Irene.

The families who lived out on Fork Mountain when Betty was growing up were mostly Campbells, Fitzgeralds, and Bradleys, as well as members of the Bryant clan. Betty remembers that there was a sawmill in the meadow below their home that was run by Mr. Pamplin Bradley.

Betty began school in the four-room Montebello School, which was located on the hill above Painter Mountain Road. She remembers starting the first grade and going barefoot into the woods to dig ginseng roots at recess. She remembers that Robert Seaman was one of the teachers at the school, and her second-grade teacher was Miss Barbara Dickie, who passed all the boys but failed all the girls that year.

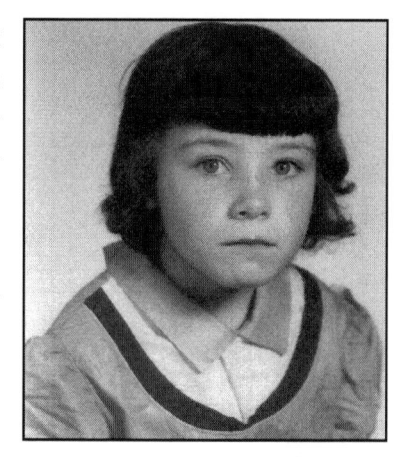

Betty at six years old when she started school

I asked what the deal was and Betty laughed and said, "I guess all us girls were such mean little devils she failed us. The other kids weren't much better. When the teacher would go outside, bigger kids would start jumping up and carrying on. Some of the older boys would set the woodshed or the outdoor toilets on fire, or they would rock the outhouse while we were in it.

"And the teacher would send us little kids down to the spring to get water. We'd put that bucket up on our shoulders, holding it with a long stick across our backs, and march up that road, carrying it back. One time, we went to get water at Nellie Campbell's house and tipped her cream over in the spring by accident. And me and Carolyn Seaman got into a fight in the second grade over some slide that went down the hill, and she pulled my hair so hard I had bald spots all over my head. It's no wonder we failed! I also remember a Campbell boy who would jump on the back of the drink truck as it geared down the hill by Homer Anderson's store, and he'd steal the bottles off the back.

"Mama packed our lunch, and it was usually biscuits. I remember Darlene Falls's mother, Vera, would pack her biscuits with persimmons on them, and I loved those, so we would trade lunches."

Betty remembers another time when she cut her foot at school, and the teacher made her put her foot in a gallon bucket so that she wouldn't get blood all over the car. The teacher drove Betty over to Doctor Kennan's office in Raphine, where he cleaned and bandaged the wound.

Although the Montebello School went up to the seventh grade, Betty repeated the second grade the next year at Fleetwood in Massies Mill. By her own admission, she did not like school, and she got her head flicked nearly every day while at Fleetwood when they had to put their heads down on the desk for a rest. "I wasn't used to no rest period, and I'd sneak my head up to look around, and the teacher would come around and pleck me on top of the head."

She remembers that some of her classmates were Darlene Falls, Larry Wheeler, Robert Humphries, Carson Bryant, and Amy Seaman. Betty went through the seventh grade at Fleetwood School and started classes at Nelson County High School, but she quit in the tenth grade to stay home and help her mother with chores around the house. There was always water to be carried up from the spring, clothes to be washed, berries and apples to be picked, gardens to be weeded, wood to be brought in, and cows to be milked. Betty said that when she was younger, she'd come home from school and wonder what her mother had done all day long. As a teenager, she got a taste of her mother's daily recipe.

The Bryants' barn

Although the Bryants had hooked up to the electricity lines, Betty said that they did not have a television, so they would walk across the field to their Uncle Dave and Aunt Kathleen Bryant's house on Saturday nights to watch *The Jackie Gleason Show*.

I asked if they had attended Mount Paran Baptist Church, since so many of their family members are buried in the church cemetery. Betty said that when they went to services, they went to Fork Mountain Baptist Church (the old Pogue's Chapel), which was closer than Mount Paran. Preacher Bateman was the pastor of the church at that time. Melvin only owned a log truck, so more than likely, the family walked to church.

The spring house from which they got their water

Although Betty is an upbeat person, she is no stranger to the sadness that comes with living on this earth. When she was nine years of age, her young nephew died in a tragic accident. Betty's older brother Glennwood and his wife, Mary, were living in the old Fork Mountain Schoolhouse located on the Bryant

The smoke house/ground cellar at the homeplace

*Fork Mountain Baptist Church; Lewis Bryant on the steps,
Betty behind him in a plaid dress*

property. Betty's daddy, Melvin, had come for a visit and was sitting in his log truck on the hill by the school. Glennwood's young son, Lewis Wilson, began climbing on one of the back tires, and Betty's brother Bobby was holding onto him, helping him climb.

The truck coasted backward, and Lewis fell off the tire, sliding under the wheel, which ran over him. He lived until they got to the hospital in Lexington, but his injuries were too severe. He died

Melvin and Lois Bryant in later years

on July 9, 1957, one month before his third birthday. Betty said she can still remember Lewis's little casket and how he was laid to rest in the cemetery at Mount Paran Church.

After Betty quit school, Margaret Grant called her about a waitressing job at Whetstone Restaurant on the Blue Ridge Parkway. Betty was just shy of her sixteenth birthday when she took the job; that's when she got to know Lester.

Lester Holbert Roberts, born May 26, 1945, was one of seven children. His parents were Walter Alderson Roberts and Agnes May Roberts, who lived in Wise, Virginia. Agnes passed away from heart problems when Lester was sixteen. In 1962, when Lester was seventeen, he went to live with his older brother in Staunton for the summer. He found work at Transit Mix Concrete, loading and unloading trucks carrying sand and gravel. Lester said, "After I got up here, I sort of just stayed and didn't go back home."

One of Lester's co-workers at the cement plant was Lemuel Bryant, Betty's cousin, and he and Lester decided to hang around together one weekend. They ended up at a truck stop on Route 11 near Greenville and bumped into Betty who, in Lester's words, "Asked me my whole life story!"

That was on a Saturday night. The next day, Lester came into Whetstone Restaurant where Betty was working. When she saw him, she told the women working with her, "There's that boy I asked all those questions to last night."

Betty walked over and asked what she could get for him, and Lester, ever the smooth operator, replied, "I'd like to have a cup of coffee with cream and sugar, but you can just stick your finger in it to sweeten it up."

At this point, I can only believe that Betty had a huge smile on her face. They began to talk, and Lester invited her to go "snipe hunting." For anyone who doesn't know what snipe hunting involves, let's just say it's a setup for a joke played on an unsuspecting person. Although they never did go hunting, the couple dated for a while.

Lester while stationed in Vietnam

    Shortly thereafter, in 1966, Lester was drafted into the army, just a few weeks after his twenty-first birthday. He left for boot camp in Fort Bragg, North Carolina, and from there, Lester was sent to mechanic's school in New Jersey. He learned to be a "wireman," which entailed climbing up poles and stringing lines. One of the men in his outfit told him that the job wouldn't be too bad if they were stationed in the states, but, overseas, he'd be a sitting duck up that pole in enemy territory.

    Lester ended up serving fourteen and a half months in Vietnam before being discharged. He came home on June 5, 1968, and returned to Staunton and his job at Transit Mix. He lived with a fellow employee, since by that time his brother had moved.

    During the time Lester was in the service, Betty had moved on and married a man by the name of Calvin Delano Cash. Calvin's parents were from Newport News, Virginia, but he was working at a plant in Stuarts Draft when they married.

    Once again, tragedy came into Betty's life. "I was married at twenty, widowed at twenty-one, and a mother at twenty-two."

The newlyweds had been living in Greenville at the time. Betty was pregnant with their first child, when they decided one Sunday morning to drive out Route 608 to a swimming lake. Calvin, Betty, her sister Phyllis, and Pete Seaman were wading along the edge. Calvin went out too far where there was suction under the water, and he began to yell for help. He went under several times, until he didn't resurface.

He died on June 30, 1968, at twenty-six years of age, leaving behind Betty and an unborn child. Betty's parents were getting older, so the decision was made to move back home and help them while awaiting the birth of her child. A daughter, Teresa, was born on February 16, 1969, and was nicknamed "Missy."

Early photo of Betty and Lester

Three years later, Betty and Lester had resumed dating and were married in the home of Preacher Giles near Fairfield on December 18, 1971. Lester became not only Betty's husband but the only father Missy has ever known.

That spring, Lester found weekend work as a caretaker on the Blue Ridge Parkway; he would pick up trash and clean the bathrooms at the various visitor centers and restaurants. In the fall months, the men would go out and cut brush and anything else that needed to be done. He stayed in that position for about ten years before becoming a mechanic at the Montebello maintenance office at milepost 29 on the Parkway.

Missy's ninth birthday: (left to right) Melinda, Gregory, Missy, and David

Lester did all the mechanical work on trucks, chippers, power saws, and lawnmowers, and he stayed in that position until his retirement in December 2008. When asked if he missed work, Lester said that he missed the men he'd worked with in the earlier years: Edgar Austin, Danny Myrtle, Elmer Fitzgerald, Saylor Coffey, Milton Bryant, and Troy Painter, as well as many others.

Lester and Betty's daughter Melinda was born on March 26, 1972. The following December, Betty's brother Gorman and his wife had a baby boy, David Lee. Because of family circumstances, Betty and

The Roberts family (August 1981)

The Bryant siblings at Lois's funeral: Gorman, Milton, Phyllis, Edgar, Frances, Bobby, Betty, and Wendell (September 8, 2001)

Lester raised David as one of their own. On August 21, 1975, their son Gregory was born, completing their family.

The family lived with Betty's parents until 1980, when Melvin and Lois gave the couple a little over four acres, and the Roberts made the home where they continue to live. Betty's father, Melvin, passed away in July 1990, and her mother, Lois, died in September 2001.

Five of Betty's brothers have also passed away: Glennwood in 1975, Bobby in 2008, Edgar and Gorman in 2009, and Milton in 2012. Four siblings still survive: Wendell, Frances, Betty, and Phyllis.

Lester and Betty's daughter Missy married Tony Weeks, and they have two children, Matthew and Jessica. Melinda married Jeremy Campbell, and they had two children, Leanna and Nathan, before Jeremy passed away. At present, David has not married. Gregory married Crystal Fitzgerald, and they also have two children, Trevor and Austin.

I asked Lester what he does now that he's retired. He laughed and said, "There is *always* something to do around here."

For many years after her mother died, Betty was the caregiver for Thelma Bradley while Thelma's daughter Gail was working. Both Lester and Betty continue to keep busy doing what mountain folks do: gardening, canning, mowing, taking care of the grandchildren, and doing things around the house.

In December 2014, the Robertses celebrated forty-three years of marriage, and I can't think of two people who get along any better. They are full of fun and good humor, and, over coffee at the kitchen table, we had a delightful afternoon, talking about family and the many memories that have been shared with the people we love.

Lester and Betty (2014)

Carl Franklin Coffey and his sidekick, Sassy

11

Carl Franklin Coffey

My introduction to Carl came much later than the rest of his family. In the early 1980s, I remember going to his mother's house on the North Fork with a group from our church to sing hymns for her. His brother Ralph and Ralph's son Jeff had cut the logs for a cabin I began building while still a single gal. When Jeff was twelve years old, I took a picture of him at his grandmother's house that was published in *Backroads* newspaper.

I had met Carl's sisters, Charlene and Elda, in years past, but it wasn't until Carl moved back home after retirement that Billy and I met him and his future wife, Debbie. We were up Coxes Creek attending Clemon and Peggy Lawhorne's pig roast when we were introduced.

The first thing I noticed was Carl's stature. He is a giant of a man, standing six feet five inches tall, but he has a quiet demeanor and much good humor. Debbie is petite and pretty and has a warm and engaging personality. They seemed like a perfect match, and the longer we've known them, the more we've realized that our first impression of their relationship was right on the money.

Carl is a successful businessman, and he is the first to say that God has blessed him abundantly. He is a humble person who doesn't brag about what he has or what type of man he is. But those around him notice his giving and generous spirit and have many nice things to say about him.

Close neighbors cannot say enough about the favors Carl has done for them over the years; how accommodating he is and how he notices what they need done, then quietly goes about doing it without fanfare or expected payment. Carl is known for how fairly he treats others and how far-reaching his hospitality extends throughout the community.

Junior Thompson is a good friend whom Carl has known for many years. Junior knew Carl as a young boy; he watched Carl grow up and took him bear hunting as a teenager. In talking with Junior, he had this to say: "Carl Coffey has done well for himself. He left home and started his own business. But with all the material success he's had, it never went to his head. He's still the same old guy. Yes, Carl is a great guy."

In talking with Carl about his lineage, I found that I already had a vast amount of information that people had sent me over the years, much of which belonged to his particular branch of Coffey genealogy. I realize that someone reading this book who lives in Alabama might not find this bit of family history as interesting as we folks who actually live here, but for the Nelson County natives who were born and raised here, it is a record for the future that may be lost if not written down now. For that reason alone, I am including what I have concerning Carl's family line so that it will not be lost.

They say if you want to know the worth of a person, ask his friends. I did, and their words reflect the love and respect they have for this special man. Enjoy Carl's story about a poor boy who left the mountains to make a better life for himself and his family, only to return to the peace and solitude of the place he's always called "home."

Carl Franklin Coffey

Carl's paternal grandfather was Benjamin Franklin Coffey, who was born on September 26, 1847, and died on September 14, 1926. Benjamin was the son of Henry B. Coffey and Polly Campbell Coffey. Carl's paternal grandmother was Elizabeth M. Fitzgerald Coffey, who was born on July 14, 1855, and died February 20, 1937. Her parents were Moses Fitzgerald and Polly Coffey Fitzgerald. Benjamin and Elizabeth are both buried in the Coffey graveyard located on North Fork Road to the left of the first bridge over the Tye River, near their homeplace.

The Benjamin Franklin Coffey family in early 1900: (top row) Zandy, Patrick, Marshall, and Aubrey; (bottom row) Benjamin, Eva, and Elizabeth (Martha, a second daughter, not pictured)

Carl's maternal grandfather was Bennett Franklin Fitzgerald, who was born August 3, 1878, and died September 4, 1960. He was the son of Martin Luther Fitzgerald (June 24, 1854–April 2, 1913) and Mary Elizabeth "Lizzie" Carr Fitzgerald (September 20, 1854–May 5, 1941). Bennett's wife, Mary Etta Fitzgerald, was born on May 9, 1880, and died on February 27, 1966. She was the daughter of Hugh Fitzgerald and Sophia Campbell Fitzgerald. They are buried in the Fitzgerald family cemetery located on Fork Mountain Road in Montebello.

Bennett and Mary Etta's daughter, Quincey Eunice, was born on September 14, 1909; she married Patrick Henry Coffey sometime in the 1920s. Patrick was born on February 20, 1879, and was thirty years older than his bride.

Pat and Quincey were Carl's parents, and the couple had four children before Pat passed away on October 19, 1948, at the age of sixty-nine. The children, by order of birth, are: Charlene Marie, born April 4, 1931; Carl Franklin, born June 2, 1940; Ralph Davis, born July 11, 1942; and Lecy Elda, born April 29, 1944. Elda was named after Leasy (Lecy) Snead Adams, the midwife who delivered most of the children in the area at that time.

Patrick and Quincey Coffey

Carl was only eight years old when his father died of a massive stroke, leaving him and his brother Ralph, age six, the "men" of the family. Carl remembers, "It was early in the morning, and I had gone to school. I didn't know anything had happened until I got home that evening, and Frank Zirkle met me out at the road and told me my dad had died. Back then, the bus stopped at the bridge, and we had to walk up the road a ways and up over the hill. There was quite a group of people up at the house, and they said my dad was putting a stick of wood in the fireplace when he had the stroke."

Although Carl was very young and can't remember exact details of his father's death, he said, "He never left the house after he died and was laid out in a coffin in the back room until the funeral," which was the tradition at that time. He does remember the hearse taking Pat's remains to Evergreen Christian Church for the funeral and afterward to the Coffey family graveyard up on the mountain across the road from their home. Carl said, "As they left the house to take my dad to the church, his little dog, Brownie, kept following the hearse. A lot of people commented on that, along with my mother."

The Coffey homeplace on the North Fork

After Pat's death, the two brothers went to work cutting, splitting, and bringing home the massive amounts of firewood the family needed for warmth and cooking purposes. "My dad had cut timber and had a few tools, but not many, because we were poor as snakes. We had a crosscut and some kind of bow saw we used to cut wood with. It was extremely hard to keep wood, because we had no way of bringing it down to the yard. We had no vehicle, and although my dad had a horse, after he died, my mother gave it to my grandfather, because we weren't big enough to handle it.

"I remember Lena Zirkle, who was a neighbor, was always so good to us. She lost her husband about a year after my dad died and never remarried, raising her four children alone, just like my mother. I always respected and honored her.

Carl and the family dog, Brownie

The Coffey family: (back row) Charlene, Ralph, and Quincey; (front row) Elda and Carl

"It was rough living, and we struggled along, but, actually, it was fun. I would act like a horse, and Ralph and I had this wooden thing that we'd hook up and drag it out of the woods. We burned wood exclusively; no other heat. We had a fireplace, and that's what heated the whole house. We had a room that was supposed to be the family room, but it was turned into a bedroom because that's where most of the heat was. After my dad died, my mother and all us kids slept in the same bed for the longest time.

"All our meals were cooked on a wood cookstove that had a warming closet on top. It was pretty nice to come home from school and grab a warm biscuit and go squirrel hunting. My dad had a gun, but I don't remember what ever happened to that gun. When Ralph and I were ten and twelve years old, somebody bought us a .22 rifle, and we used that. Then Charlene's husband, James Morris, and another relative gave us a shotgun when we were fourteen and twelve years old, and that's what we used to hunt with. Before that, we'd borrow a gun from Elmer Carr and use that to hunt. We didn't have many bullets; Mom would go down to Junior Hatter's store and buy ten .22 bullets or five shotgun shells and give us one or two, and we knew we better bring something home!

"We had three gardens, one down by the road and two at home. Basically, we raised everything we ate. We grew lots of potatoes, beans, tomatoes, corn, and cabbage. We usually raised a couple of hogs that were butchered and we ate on, but the hams were always sold to get a little extra money. Mostly they were sold to my uncle, Aubrey Coffey, who was a minister in Logan, West Virginia. Some of the hog meat, like sausage, spareribs, and backbones were canned. The rest of the hog was salted down and kept.

"We had a few chickens and one milk cow, but eventually it died, and then we didn't even have milk. All of our water was dipped up out of the creek and brought to the house in buckets for washing, which was done with an old scrub board. In the winter, you had to break the ice to get a drink of water. We didn't have electricity until I was about seventeen years old.

"Later on, we got help. Elmer Carr, Boston and Tommy Taylor came to get in wood. As we got older, they would come and help us log. Ralph and I started logging when we were quite little. That's when we and Lester Fitzgerald raised an ox named "Mike," and that was our method of plowing the garden and hauling in the wood. It takes a lot of patience to train an ox.

"Mike," the ox the boys used for logging

We didn't have a yoke to put on him, and the top of Mike's neck was bigger than the bottom, so we took a horse collar and turned it upside down and used it that way."

I remember talking with Ralph when I published a logging issue of *Backroads*, and he had told me how he and Carl and Lester would cut logs and drag them from the woods down to a landing with the ox. They were so little that other men were hired to take the logs to Bland Lawhorne's sawmill, and the boys would pay the men out of their earnings. Carl and Lester cut logs with handsaws; they didn't get a gasoline-powered chain saw until they were older teens.

Carl laughed at the memory of Boston and Tommy Taylor, who were the first ones on the North Fork to get a chain saw. "They bought a McCullough saw that you'd pull on for a half a day to get it started. Ralph and I bought a used Homelite that started just like that [snaps fingers], and we were the top of the crew for a while."

Carl continued, "After Dad died, we were extremely poor and were struggling to get by. My mom and we kids worked in July and August at the orchards, picking peaches for fifty cents an hour—ten hours for five dollars. I remember a fairly large peach orchard on Campbell's Mountain Road that I picked at [Andy Coffey's orchard]. We worked for Sam Saunders, S. P. Bethel, and J. S. Jordan.

"In elementary school, I was large for my age, and Walter Hoffman would take me after school and on weekends to pick peaches at his orchard on Dickie Road that I own now. Mom worked for these same orchards picking apples after we had gone back to school. At that time, Nelson County was just a huge apple growing concern in this area, and there were orchards everywhere.

"Shortly after my dad died, we were on welfare. We had to supplement that by earning what we could. For my mother and all the kids, we got thirteen dollars and some change each month [from the government]. From the late 1940s to 1952, that's what we got. In 1952, they raised it to forty-two dollars and some change, and I can remember my mother crying like she'd been whipped, because we were going to live so much better. I still have that little piece of paper that shows us getting that increase."

As children, Carl and his siblings attended the Fleetwood School that, at the time, had elementary grades one through seven and high school grades nine through twelve. Carl said that some of the bus drivers during his school years were: Wilson Lawhorne, Lila Campbell, Parrish Strickland, and Carl himself; he drove a bus in his junior/senior year. Carl's teachers were Mrs. Powell for first grade, Mrs. Dodd for second grade, Mrs. Turpin for third grade, Mrs. Crockett for fourth grade, and Mrs. Beard for fifth grade.

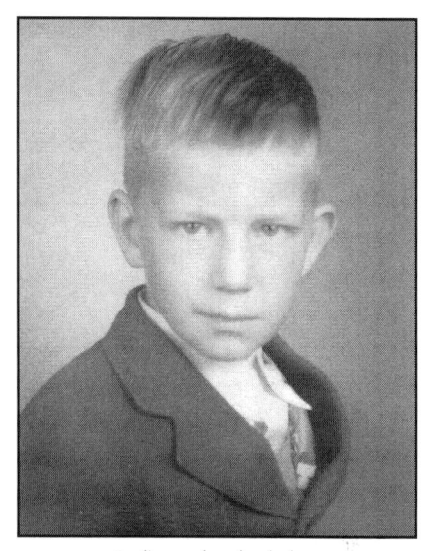

Carl's grade school photo

In 1956, the consolidated high school was built, and that's where Carl attended the upper grades, graduating in 1960. He added, "One time my mom got sick, and I quit when I was a sophomore to help her. I had to, because there was no one else to help her. It was at Christmastime, and I didn't go back for the rest of that year. It's a thousand wonders that I went back and finished, but my mother was the driving force for me returning, and I guess I had enough foresight to know I needed to go back.

"Because I didn't start school until I was seven years old and then quit for a year when Mom was sick, I had just turned twenty when I graduated. Bo Zirkle and I were among the few that graduated around there; most of my peers quit when, or before, they were sixteen. That was the age when you could drop out and the truant officer wouldn't come looking for you."

After graduation, Carl worked for about a year around home, but in 1961, a man by the name of Arnie Coffey came

Carl's graduation picture (1960)

to their house. He wanted to know if Carl and Ralph might like to come and work with him on a project in northern Virginia. The project was clearing land for a water impoundment dam that Redd and Warren Contractors were building along Goose Creek in Loudoun County.

So the two brothers and Richard Carr left to work in northern Virginia. They obtained lodging in a boarding house for twelve dollars a week, which Carl said included "breakfast, dinner, and a cheese sandwich for lunch . . . *very thin* sliced cheese." Ralph and Richard stayed for about a month before becoming homesick and heading back to the mountains they called home.

Carl said, "I toughed it out and stayed on. I was making a dollar and twenty-five cents an hour, which was good money back then, running a chain saw cutting bushes and trees. By then I was good with a chain saw . . . real good. It wasn't long before one of the equipment operators quit, and I began running a loader and a new bulldozer and got pretty familiar with them.

"My pay went up, and, before I knew it, I was the only one out there clearing

Arnie Coffey, the man who got Carl the job in Loudoun County.

Carl at the Loudoun County boarding house

the property. I cleared both sides down to where the water was going to be, about five miles long. You didn't have to push the stumps out because when the dam was finished, they would be about thirty feet under the water.

"By that time, Ralph and I had a GMC truck, and I'd load it up with the large logs I'd cut during the week and drive home on Friday night and drive back to work on Sunday. That solved our firewood and money problems. By that time, we had bought a horse and could drag wood to the house. We put a new tin roof on the house, replacing the wooden shingles, and put a tin heater in the dining room."

Carl worked on the dam project for about two years; then Bill Warren, one of the partners who owned Redd and Warren Contractors, died. After Bill's death, his wife asked Carl to stay on and finish the work, which he did. By the time Mr. Redd had also died, the Warrens' son, Don, had graduated from college. He formed a new company called Centerville Construction, and Carl stayed on with them until October 1963. That's when he was drafted into the army; he spent the next two years serving our country.

After basic training, Carl had been hoping to go to Fort Belvoir, which was the engineering area of the army where all the heavy equipment was kept. But Uncle Sam had other ideas, and Carl ended up becoming a medic. When he finished his medic training, he was sent to Maryland, where he spent the rest of his military career participating in "Operation White Coat," a germ-warfare research program.

Carl said that it was a great tour of duty; he went to work at 8:30 a.m., got off at 11:00 for lunch, went back at 1:00 p.m., and finished at 4:30. After all the hard physical work up to that point in his life, the army position seemed like a vacation.

Carl and his buddy had new cars, and since Hood College was close by, there were girls everywhere. Carl smiled as he told me, "I enjoyed my tour, let me tell you!" His pay was sixty-four dollars a month. Haircuts were a dollar, laundry was a dollar, and two dollars were appropriated for other essentials, leaving him sixty dollars a month to live on. Deduct fifty dollars for the car payment, and Carl was having the time of his life on ten dollars a month. Carl said, "You could spend your last dime and still get three meals a day and clean sheets twice a week—livin' large!"

During the time Carl was in the army in Maryland, Linda Campbell was attending college there. In earlier years, Carl had worked for Linda's dad, Harold, and the young people had gone to school together. They began dating and married on June 5, 1966. They had two biological children: Laurie Alice, who was born on August 13, 1972, and Carla Elizabeth, born November 20, 1974. The couple also adopted a son, Kevin, who was born on August 19, 1975, when he was a year old.

When Carl got out of the army, he went back to northern Virginia. He continued working for Centerville Construction for about a year, then the company went under. Before the company folded, Carl had been hired to run a track loader for the S. O.

Carl with his nephew, Jeff Coffey, and daughter Laurie

Carl with his three children: Carla, Kevin, and Laurie

Jennings Company, which installed large pipe, such as culverts and sanitation pipes. He eventually made foreman on the pipe crew, getting a raise in salary and a truck to drive.

By that time, Centerville Construction was back in business under a new name, Dulles Construction, and they offered Carl twice what he was making at Jennings. Carl couldn't turn that down, so he went back to work for them. Four years later, the company went broke for the second time, and Carl learned a valuable lesson in what *not* to do in the construction business.

In July 1974, Carl and his good friend and co-worker, Kevin Aiken, and five other people from Dulles got together and started their own company, Phoenix Development Corporation. Kevin and Carl became partners and have worked together for about forty-five years now. They took over the jobs that Dulles Construction had started and began getting new clients of their own, building a reputation for being honest and hard-working. That type of business always gets noticed, and, before long, the company began to grow and prosper.

By 1985, Phoenix Development had between 250 and 300 employees. Things were going along smoothly until early

The Phoenix Development Corporation

1990, when an economic downturn began in the area. It was also at this time that Carl and his wife were going through a divorce. The marriage ended in December of that year. At one point, Carl said he thought that he'd lose the business, but he went to the First Virginia Bank and pleaded with them not to foreclose on them.

Carl said, "And they didn't. They stuck with us, and we pulled through. By the end of 1991 and the early part of 1992, things started turning around, and the economy rebounded. With a small business loan, coupled with a bank loan, we were able to buy twenty acres with a large construction facility that was empty because of an earlier foreclosure."

Carl said that it was a perfect setup; the building had plenty of office space, as well as a huge shop with nine sixty-foot bays. With this purchase, Phoenix Development was pushed to a whole new level, being able to compete with other contractors. Carl adds, "We had good workers, a good pay scale, and a benefit package to keep them."

Debbie Kibler was one of the employees hired in 1994 to take care of the paperwork for employee health benefits, but she left after six months, because she didn't feel there was enough work to justify getting a paycheck. In the meantime, the lady doing

The Coffey homeplace today

payroll had to leave because of health reasons, and Debbie was talked into coming back.

In the fall of 1994, Carl made a trip back to the mountains to attend his mother's funeral. Quincey, who had died on October 6, was laid to rest next to her husband, Patrick, in the family cemetery along the North Fork of the Tye River. Two years later, on June 10, 1996, Carl's brother, Ralph, was buried there also. Carl and Jeff, Ralph's son, now own the homeplace together.

Carl explained that, originally, his grandparents lived in a house up Panel Branch, but that house had burned down, so they'd built a new home. After Carl's parents were married, they lived in Charlie Coffey's cabin, which is still standing and now is owned by Carleton and Libby Coffey. When Carl's grandparents died, Quincey and Patrick moved into the homeplace where Carl and his siblings grew up.

In December 2001, Phoenix Development was sold to a competitor. Carl said that at the time of the sale, "We had five hundred employees, as well as four of the original seven men who started with the company. The company had numerous pieces of clearing, earth-moving, pipe installation, and other miscellaneous equipment, including a lot of trucks. The Lord just blessed us unbelievably."

The company did it all: building highways; laying out subdivisions and housing developments; sewer, water, and storm drainage work; laying asphalt; and curbing gutters. Debbie continued to work as the payroll secretary until September 2003, and Carl stayed on at the company as a consultant until

A large fleet of Phoenix dump trucks

December 2003, when he "retired." The word "retirement," I've found, does not mean quitting work but instead doing the work you like.

Carl and Kevin have continued their partnership in a successful mulch/compost business that Phoenix owned in northern Virginia. Years ago, they'd bought forty acres that backs up to the boundary fence at Dulles Airport. Part of the land was sold off, but almost twenty-six acres was kept as a place to bring old stumps and wood to be ground up.

When Phoenix Development Corporation was sold, the sale did not include this part of the company; Carl and Kevin still own it, but the company basically runs itself. It is now called Loudoun Composting, and it takes in all the grass clippings, yard waste, and leaves from the surrounding counties to be ground up. The company has two trademark products that it sells, compost and leaf mulch, both of which are sold to landscape and nursery businesses almost faster than they can produce it. Loudoun employs twelve people, including Carl's daughter Laurie, who is the company accountant, and Kevin's son-in-law, Tim Hutchison, the general manager.

When Carl "officially" retired in December 2003, he decided, like so many people who were raised up in Nelson County, to move back "home" to the mountains. He looked at several places before settling on a beautiful piece of land close to Massies Mill. It's called the Flat Farm and was established in 1820. The two hundred–acre farm needed some TLC, so a lot of work was done before taking up residence in August 2004. Carl also bought a hundred acres across the road that had originally belonged to Walter Hoffman, the man who'd hired Carl to pick apples as a young man.

On June 18, 2013, Billy had the honor of marrying Carl to Debbie Kibler at their farm. The couple, who had been going together for a long time, tied the knot with the beauty of the Blue Ridge Mountains as a backdrop. It is obvious

Carl and Debbie on their wedding day (June 18, 2013)

that they are a happy couple, and they share their home and hospitality with those around them. When they married, the Coffeys had a combined family that includes Carl's three children as well as Debbie's two children, Brad and Katie, from a previous marriage. Between them, they also have twelve grandchildren.

These days, Carl and Debbie keep busy around the farm. They have 125 brood cows and make vast amounts of hay to feed them, and there are horses and dogs in abundance, including Carl's guard dog and sidekick, "Sassy." The Coffeys have several employees to help with the farm work. Carl continues to enjoy the sport of bear hunting and when asked who he hunts with, Billy and I smile at familiar folks and their bear-hunting nicknames: Jethro, Ellie Mae, Polkberry, Apple Picker, Oz, Wino, Shue Creek, Mexico, String Bean, Trigger,

Bean Head, Ugly, Bull Rider, Leggs, and many more. Good folks. Good company. Good hunters.

As the morning wore on, and we had just about finished talking, Carl volunteered that he's had a pretty colorful life. "I've done a lot of things and been a lot of places. I've met two presidents—both Bushes." Carl said that met one of them when he he was dating a Secret Service lady, and he'd escorted her to the Inaugural Ball.

"I met Robert Duvall several times and went to one of his parties. I got to meet Elizabeth Taylor and some governors and been to most of the states and to Europe a few times."

With everything he's done, I asked Carl why he decided to move back home. His answer didn't surprise me.

Carl and his dog, Blade

"Why, there's no place like Nelson County. It's one of the well-kept secrets of all time. It's such a blissful, beautiful place. Everybody waves to you with that two-finger wave. I had the best childhood ever and didn't know we were poor. I wouldn't change my upbringing for anything. It made good, sound, solid people. It was a good life. We found things to do. We'd go down to the river and hop rocks to see who could get the furthest without getting their feet wet, or we'd go ginseng hunting. Kids now don't know anything about nature. Nature is God's second book. You go out in nature, and there are so many things to learn."

Debbie told how Carl, as a child, would pack some food in a knapsack and take off for a week, exploring. When asked where he went, Carl smiled and said, "Wherever my feet would take me."

Carl and Debbie at the Flat Farm (2015)

Sarah Jane Hatter Urbanski

12

Sarah Jane Hatter Urbanski

What a treat to finally get to meet Sarah and her husband, Ed. She and her daughter, Kris Gembara, used to subscribe to *Backroads* newspaper, and I remember sticking their mailing labels on the newspapers and sending them off to where they lived in Illinois. Then one day, Kris was visiting her mom, who had already moved back to Virginia, and happened to come to Mountain Top Christian Church where I was worshipping that day. When she introduced herself, the name suddenly struck a chord, and we had a hug-fest at finally meeting after all the years of corresponding.

Kris and I became fast friends, and, whenever she would visit, we'd go on great mountain adventures. I introduced her to many of the people she had read about through the pages of *Backroads* and found she was related to many of them. When plans were made for *Mountain Folk*, I knew I wanted to interview her mom, who started out living in Love, then later moved across the mountain to Spruce Creek.

Sarah accepted, and when I went to her home, I liked her immediately and found we'd had a lot of similar life experiences. Sarah is a pretty, petite woman with a sparkling personality and great sense of humor. We had a delightful afternoon talking about how she grew up in the Blue Ridge Mountains of Virginia.

─────

Sarah Jane was one of twelve children born to Saylor Franklin Hatter and Pearl May Coffey Hatter, who were married in Bedford, Virginia, on September 21, 1933. The Hatter side of the family came from the Love area, and Saylor's mother was Willie Hatter, who later married Leslie Allen. Pearl's family came from Durham's Run, near Montebello, and her parents were Dellie Coffey and Mittie Hatter Coffey.

The twelve Hatter siblings, by order of birth, were: Wilford (who died young), Charlene, Austin, Alton, Shirley, Jerry, Jackie, Wilbert, Sarah, a set of twins, and Roland, who was always called "Button." It is thought that many of the children were born in Bedford, where the Hatters were married, but Sarah and her brother Wilbert were born in a log cabin that stood on the property at the base of Love Mountain where Bobby Henderson and Russell Lowery now live. The story goes that Saylor Hatter got the place from a man who needed bail money to get someone out of jail.

Sarah's mother, Pearl Hatter

Sarah Jane was born on May 15, 1944, and she said that from the firstborn all the way down the line, there was only a one-year gap between each child, except for a four-year space between her and Button when the twins died. The family attended Mountain View Mennonite Church at the base of the mountain, and the twins are buried there in the church cemetery.

Sarah was still a baby when the family moved into her grandparents' cabin in Page Holler, just a short distance from where she was born. At this time, there were eight children still living; Button had not yet been born. As a child, Sarah said that she slept in a blue baby crib that was situated under a window in a room off the kitchen. She can remember looking out the window and seeing pink blossoms on a peach tree growing outside the cabin.

Sarah's father, Saylor, making sport with his pistol

She said, "I can remember a lot of stuff back before I was a year old, like being wrapped up in a blanket and my dad carrying me to church and crossing three creeks. I can still remember seeing how clear the water was and the pebbles on the bottom. Coming home from church, I was looking up and could see the sun coming down through the trees."

When Sarah was older, all the children slept in the open, upstairs loft on straw tick mattresses. Pearl sewed

Pearl with six of her children: (top row) Shirley, Sarah Jane, and Jackie; (bottom row) Austin, Roland, and Wilbert (1950s)

the mattress covers out of colorful cotton feed sacks, and they were then stuffed with straw.

The Hatters grew all their own food and kept hogs to butcher in the fall, but Sarah said that at one point, her father left and went to Illinois to work on a farm to earn extra money and "hoboed" back and forth. Later, Saylor acquired a Model T Ford and found permanent employment as a weaver at the Crompton Factory in Waynesboro, carpooling with a neighbor, Willie Henderson.

Pearl canned fruit and vegetables for her large family, and they hunted possum, squirrel, groundhog, raccoon, and bears for meat, to supplement the domestic animals that were kept and butchered.

Sarah said, "I can remember Wilbert and I were roaming around outside when he was about four and I was three, and we saw a cow up on this hill, having a calf; and we were so scared, because she had this thing hanging out of her and was bawling, and her eyes were real big. We ran home and told my mom, and she told us the cow was just trying to have a baby.

"Another time, my brothers Alton and Jerry were out hunting rabbits with a bow and arrow Alton had made, and they saw a large bear in the woods, so they ran back to tell Dad, and Dad came out and shot the bear. When they dragged her out, she had two little cubs on her that we raised and fed with a bottle. One was a boy and the other was a girl, and we named them Jack and Jill.

"We kept them until they started to get mean, and then my dad had to chain them up, because my mom would be out in the yard churning butter, and they would come up and take the churn away from her. She'd run in the house, and the bears would lick up all the cream. My mother would send me out to get wood chips to start the fire with, and I'd throw little rocks at them just to hear them growl. Later on, someone from a zoo came and got them."

Sarah was around four years old when the family moved from Page Holler to a house in Love. It was up the mountain on the main road and was bought from Carl Hewitt, Sr. Carl had built the home from lumber that had been salvaged from the disused Dunkard Church at the top of the mountain. This home was later sold to Hallie Henderson, who raised her three sons, Joe, Melvin, and Marvin, there (see chapter 6).

Sarah Jane said that the Hewitt house was much nicer than the cabin in Page Holler; it had a living room, dining room, kitchen, two bedrooms downstairs, and several bedrooms upstairs. Although the house didn't have electricity or indoor plumbing, there was a bold (continuously flowing) spring outside the back door that provided the family's water.

Wilbert, Jackie, and Sarah at the house in Love

Sarah said that they had two large chicken houses where pullets were raised for a local hatchery. The chickens were watered by a gravity-fed system that ran directly from the spring into the chicken houses. She laughs at the memory of going in to feed the chickens, listening to the loud cheeping of the birds, and clapping her hands, which brought complete silence for a few seconds before the chickens resumed their cheeping.

She started the first grade at Hall School, a Mennonite-run school that was located halfway between Stuarts Draft and Waynesboro. Sarah said, "When we were small, we always went barefoot, even to school. We got one pair of shoes each year."

Sarah recalls the first time she saw indoor plumbing. "When I went to the first grade, the school had indoor plumbing, with a line of sinks on one side and a line of commodes and paper on the other wall. I had no idea what they were for until recess when another girl went in there, and I saw what was going on. I remember the cabin in the holler had newspapers tacked up on the walls to keep out drafts, and my sister Charlene taught us younger kids to read those newspapers before we even started school."

For second grade and halfway through third, Sarah attended the Stuarts Draft Elementary School. When she was eight years old, the family decided to move to a remote mountain location at the head of Spruce Creek in Nelson County.

When asked why they had moved, Sarah said, "I never figured it out, because my mom loved living at the house in Love. It was right on the road, and she had people coming in to visit, like Willie and Sarah Henderson, Effie Quick, and Aunt Lottie Hatter, who lived up the road. Maybe my dad thought the boys would get in trouble or something, so he bought a hundred acres and a house on Spruce Creek from Cliff Truslow. At that time, Charlene had gotten married, so there were eight kids—five boys and three girls—when we moved there."

In transition, the family lived a short time with Saylor's mother and her husband, Leslie Allen, in a two-story log cabin before moving into the home bought from Cliff Truslow.

Sarah said that Saylor and Pearl grew a large garden on the land that included a section of the mountain called "Tomato Hill" that they had cleared to plant tomatoes. The ripe tomatoes were eaten, canned, or sold to Mulford Camp-

Pearl and Saylor Hatter at the Love home (1950s)

Willie and Leslie Allen's cabin on Spruce Creek as it looks today

bell and B. C. Small, who ran country stores in the vicinity. Huckleberries, wild strawberries, and blackberries were picked in the summer months; some were eaten fresh, others canned for later use.

Sarah Jane said that, as a girl, she was an outdoorsy tomboy and loved going coon hunting with her brothers. "I never killed one; I didn't like killing them. But I liked being outside, listening to the leaves rustle and the creek making a hum. I hand-fished in Spruce Creek until we learned if you shot a .22 rifle into the water, it would stun the fish, and when they floated up to the top, you could get them.

Sarah's dad carrying water from the spring

"I hunted with my brother Wilbert; we shot squirrels and anything that moved, because when you have eight kids, they gotta eat! We hunted back on Pryor's Camp, the Fortune place, and at Black Rock, which is now part of Wintergreen.

"When you were growing up, you didn't think of your life being hard, because you didn't know any different. But sometimes now, when I'm putting a load of clothes in the washer or dryer, I think of what my mom had to do to wash clothes with a scrub board, until my dad bought her a gasoline-powered washing machine. I thought it was a great toy, and Wilbert, Jackie, and I had a lot of fun with it. We would get a big board and put it behind the wringer, while Jackie and I put kitchen knives through it and watched as they popped out and stuck in the board. But I liked the way I lived. I think it made me strong. It was always quiet.

"The first piece of store-bought bread I ever had was in the third grade when I ate lunch in the school cafeteria. They had big slices of it on the table, and I was pigging out on it—thought it was the best thing I ever had! I was fifteen years old when I saw my first movie in Lovingston, and it was a cowboy movie. I was about thirteen when I went to town for the first time, to a carnival. I was so fascinated with all the lights, and after that, whenever I went coon hunting and sat on top of the mountain looking down on all the lights, I would say, 'Someday I'm going to live where there are a lot of lights!'

"As children, we played games like hide-and-seek and crack the whip. My dad had one horse by the name of Brock that he farmed with, and we had chickens, a few cows, and all kinds of hunting dogs. My Grandmother Mittie would come and stay with us during the summers. When it was hot, we would climb out of the upstairs windows and lay on top of the porch roof.

"We took baths in the creek and washed with lye soap that my mother made. We made apple butter and boiled down cracklins after the hogs were butchered. I always felt sorry for my mom—stuck back in the mountains, and she never drove. One time, she went to Waynesboro and was going to get a job washing dishes in a restaurant, and I got out the Sears Roebuck catalog and started looking to see what I was going to get, but my dad wouldn't let her work, so I took the catalog and put it back in the outhouse."

Sarah Jane said that some of the other people living on Spruce Creek at the time were members of the Allen, Truslow, Campbell, Hughes, and Napier families. Like most people living on the creek, the Hatters attended Wintergreen Christian Church, located at the bottom of their road.

The Hatter homeplace at the head of Spruce Creek

Sarah went to the third through the seventh grades at the Rockfish School and graduated from Nelson County High School in June 1962. She went into the marine corps in September. When I asked why she'd wanted to enlist in the military, Sarah Jane said, "I knew there was something out there. In grade school, I used to read a lot, taking books from the school library over the winter so I could read about all these different places. I told Dad that someday I'd like to see the Blue Ridge Mountains that I read about, and he started to laugh and

Sarah Jane at age sixteen

asked me, 'Don't you know where you're at?' How did I know that's where we lived?

"All five of my brothers went to the marines after high school, and Wilbert and I joined the same day, signing up in Richmond. I had my basic training at Parris Island, South Carolina."

I inquired if basic training was hard and asked if she had seen the movie, *Private Benjamin*. Sarah laughed out loud, saying it was *much* worse than the movie, adding, "It was really hard, but as long as you kept your mouth shut, you got along good. The only time you got to sit down was when you were in class, sitting down to eat, or in the bathroom; you were always moving, running. But I liked the marines and feel every woman should go in the military before college to learn discipline."

Sarah Jane in her marine barracks (1963)

After basic, Sarah remained at Parris Island, staying there the whole two years she was in the marine corps. She worked as a cost accounting clerk for motor transport, keeping track of how many hours each man spent on each vehicle and how many batteries and parts were used in a month.

Sarah met her first husband, Danny Suchanek, who was also a marine at Parris Island, when he called for another girl. Sarah picked up the phone, because no one else was there. They got to talking, he came over to meet her, and they started dating. The couple dated for about two and a half years before Danny was discharged and went home to Chicago. Six months later,

Sarah was discharged with the rank of lance corporal and went to Chicago also. She lived with Danny's grandmother for about a year before the couple married in 1966 at Saint Gall Catholic Church.

Danny found work as a mail clerk at the Crane Company, and Sarah became a secretary at the Westinghouse Corporation.

Sarah and Ed's wedding (1972)

Their first child was born on February 22, 1967, a daughter named Kristin Susan. Soon after her birth, Danny left the marriage. The couple tried to make another go of it, but they ended up divorcing when Kris was four years of age.

Sarah continued to work. About six months after the divorce, she met her current husband, Ed Urbanski, at a laundromat they both used. They went out for coffee a few times, then dated for six months before marrying at City Hall on November 18, 1972.

Ed had been born on May 19, 1934, and was ten years older

Sue, Rich, Joe, Kenny, and Kris at Kris's kindergarten graduation (1973)

than Sarah when they wed. He was a widower with four children: Joe (13), Richie (12), Susie (11), and Kenny (6). Kris was five when Ed formally adopted her, changing her last name to Urbanski.

Ed was a manager at the International Harvester Tractor Company, and, after it closed, he found work as a bus driver for the Chicago Transit Authority.

The Urbanski kids: Sue, Kenny, Kris, Rich, and Joe (1995)

In 1975, Pearl was still living back at the homeplace when she died from complications of diabetes. Sarah said that when she came home for the funeral, she "saw" her mother sitting in her favorite chair in the living room, and her little dog would not let Sarah approach her mother. She says, "I think I saw my mother's ghost."

Saylor continued to live at the homeplace until his death in 1982.

There is a great story about Kris. She was in her third year of college when the Ringling Brothers and Barnum & Bailey Circus came to Chicago for

Kris and Kenny at the Hatter homeplace on Spruce Creek

auditions. Sarah related, "I was at work, and Ed had the day off and took her to audition, and I came home from work, and Kris says, 'Ma, I'm leaving two days after Thanksgiving.' I asked where she was going, and she said she had joined the circus. I didn't think too much about it until Ed said, 'It's true. I took her to audition for dancing, and she got in.' I was so mad at him!"

Saylor and Pearl in their later years

Kris (left) practicing aerial ballet in the circus

Kris lived on a train and went to Venice, Florida, the wintering grounds for the circus. She started out as a dancer but later rode the elephants and did aerial ballet on ropes, an art form known as the Spanish Web. She stayed with the circus for about a year before returning home. She took a few more college courses, then married her husband, Brian Gembara.

By this time, Sarah Jane was working for a large insurance company that offered to pay for a college education, two semesters per year. It took her ten years to get her degree, but Sarah graduated in 1995, at fifty years of age, with a double major in psychology and sociology.

She then found employment as a paralegal in a law office. Sarah and Ed lived in Chicago for forty-two years. In 2008, Ed had a heart attack that required open heart surgery, and Sarah retired in 2009. Through the years, the Urbanskis had gone many times to visit Sarah's large family; after Ed's heart problems, the couple began to talk about moving to Virginia.

All five of the children were already established in Illinois when Ed and Sarah made the move in May 2010. Plans were being made to put up a home on Spruce Creek, where Sarah Jane had inherited several acres of land, but in 2011, Ed suffered a stroke. They decided to move to Waynesboro, instead, closer to drug stores, doctors, and the hospital.

Sarah's college graduation photo

The Urbanskis have been married for forty-three years. In addition to their five children, they now have eight grandchildren and six great-grandchildren. Seven of the original twelve Hatter children still survive: Charlene, Shirley, Jerry, Jackie, Wilbert, Sarah Jane, and Button.

The Spruce Creek homeplace is still in the family. Charlene's son, Frankie Lowery, his sister Wanda Mays, and her husband now own it. Button and his wife, Kathy, live just down the road from the homeplace. Sarah Jane gave the two acres that had been left to her to Kris, making her daughter one very happy woman, because even though she wasn't raised on Spruce Creek, her heart is strongly tied to it.

Sarah Jane and Ed in the 1990s

In years past, Sarah Jane was an avid writer of poetry, and she gave me a poem to include at the end of her chapter. Anyone who has been through an ice storm like this will appreciate Sarah's descriptive words that capture the storm's raw beauty.

As the interview came to a close, I thought it so perfect that Sarah Jane got her wish to move back home and be surrounded by family and the Blue Ridge Mountains.

Sarah Jane and Ed at their Waynesboro home (2014)

"Memory of an Ice Storm"

I awoke in the woods one early morning, to a cold silence I had not known.
Something had happened during the night,
The trees and small brown shrubs were given a thin coat of frozen life.

I had never seen an ice storm, nor the effects it gave.
I sat up, stared all around,
Even the trunks of the trees were slick and shining like glass.

The sun was peeking over the east ridge, I watched till it was in full view,
Dreary this morning, and frightening, too.

The sun finally reached the trees in front of me,
Beaming off rainbow reflections of reds, pinks, yellows, greens, and blues.

I heard the noise; the warmth of the sun hitting the cold ice,
Snapping, crackling, and popping like Rice Krispies.

In a short time the ice fell to the ground,
Putting me back in my world with the winter colors of grays and browns.

Forest, Eva, Saylor, and Johnny Coffey, Love, Virginia

William Harrison Thompson, Jr.

13

William Harrison Thompson, Jr.

I'm not sure where I first met "Junior" Thompson. In fact, until the day I interviewed him, I never even knew his given name. He has always simply been "Junior" to me, and probably to many others. He is a well-known personality in Nelson County and is related to nearly everyone living here. He is very involved in county activities and is about the most community-minded person you could ever meet.

Because he's worked at the funeral home in Roseland for so many years, I guess I got to know Junior at one of the services held in the area. He is a warm and compassionate man and has the unique ability to comfort those who are grieving the loss of their loved ones. He is one of those people who always looks for the positive side of life, and it doesn't take long when talking with him to know that he is a deeply religious man who lives his faith by the way he treats others.

The day I drove over to his Piney River home for the interview, the sky was a beautiful October blue, and the golden leaves of autumn were gently falling from the trees on Campbell's Mountain Road, making a patchwork of color in front of me. It was a perfect fall day, and Junior and his daughter, Karen, were the perfect hosts as we sat and talked about Junior's growing up years. At age eighty-five, he had a lot to say, and, after looking at life through the eyes of a very wise man, I came away with a renewed sense of hope for humanity. You will, too.

❦

Junior was the first of six children born to William Harrison Thompson, Sr., and Irene Ursula Wood Thompson. He came into the world on November 13, 1929, with the help of his maternal grandmother, "Granny Sue," who was the midwife attending the birth.

Junior says, "I was born about two weeks after the stock market crashed and am a product of the Great Depression. My mother always said, 'You were part of the cause; they knew you were coming!'"

Edward Beauregard was born next, exactly two years to the day that Junior was born, on November 13, 1931. Junior gave him the nickname "Buzz" because, as a child, he could not pronounce "brother." The name stuck, and Edward went by Buzz for the rest of his life. Junior said, "We were real close, and everyone called us the Thompson Twins, born two years apart."

Another son, Calvin Delano, was born on July 20, 1933. The Thompson's first daughter, Susie Rebecca ("Becky") came on December 24, 1935, and was named after her maternal grandmother, Susie Wood. Bobby Winston was born in July 1941, and the last girl, Joanne Elizabeth, was born on September 7, 1944, fourteen years after Junior. Of the six, Junior and his two sisters are the only surviving siblings, and he likes to tease Becky by saying that she is his "oldest sister."

Junior's father was one of ten children raised in a log cabin that was located on the Little Mountain range. Junior's paternal grandfather, Henry Harrison Thompson, died before Junior was born. Junior's paternal grandmother was the former Elizabeth Massie, who went by the name of "Bessie"; she never remarried after her husband died.

William Harrison Thompson, Jr.

209

Henry Harrison Thompson's family; Junior's dad is in top row, fourth from the left

The Thompson cabin homeplace on Little Mountain;
Junior is the little boy in black at the front of the car (1932)

Junior's mother's family was from the little village of Woodson, just past Lowesville, close to the Piney River Baptist Church. Irene was raised in a large white farmhouse, and that's where Junior was born and raised. Later, his parents moved down to Lowesville, but, he says, "We went back every weekend and every holiday on that farm."

Junior's maternal grandmother, Susie, was first married to Edward Columbus Wood, who died of cancer sometime in the 1920s, when cancer was not a well-known disease. Susie then married Beauregard Johnson Wood, and although the man was Junior's step-grandfather, Junior said, "As the first grandchild, I was his fair-haired boy. He took me everywhere he went; fishing and hunting on the farm. Every picture that was taken, if *he* was in it, *I* was in it!"

When asked what it was like when he was growing up, Junior smiled and said, "Great. The happiest days of my life were spent on the farm. We worked, and I'll tell you, I've lived a long and diversified life. I'm nearly eighty-five years old and am not ashamed that I'm a country boy and know how to work—to bring water in from the spring; bring in wood; milk the cow; feed the chickens, hogs, and the horses. My grandfather had four black horses, and somewhere I have a picture of me and my brother Buzz, my uncle Edward, my grandfather, and a cousin sitting on those horses, getting ready to go to the field.

"I know how to scratch a livin' out of the ground and how to raise my meat. I butchered hogs and beef and learned how to cure it. My brother Buzz and I used to butcher hogs for the community when we were young. I like simple things, and basically I'm a country boy at heart, and I still love the land. I've been a lab technician, a front-line medic in Korea; I've served an apprenticeship as an industrial mechanic, and I am an iron worker by trade and have been fabricating steel my whole life."

As a young boy, Junior attended a little school in Lowesville for the first two years, riding a bus that was driven by Wil-

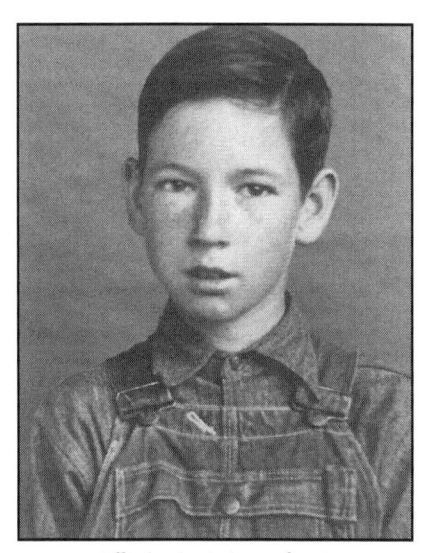

Clifford School photo of Junior at ten years of age

bert Campbell. He remembers studying his lessons by a coal oil lamp. When his parents made a move across Piney River to Amherst County, he began going to the school in Clifford, which was a little white weatherboard building then. During his second year, a new brick schoolhouse was constructed, and he finished the year there. At this point in our conversation, Junior recalled something that they did back then that he said was pretty unique.

"You couldn't do it now without an order from the United States Supreme Court, but back then, on Friday evenings, my brother and I would get on Mr. Harvey's bus at Clifford and ride up to Temperance School where we'd get off and board the bus Wilbert Campbell drove, and we'd ride back up to my grandparents' house and spend the weekend. On Monday morning, we'd do it again in reverse! Nothing was ever said, and you didn't have to have an excuse."

For the next five years, Junior went to Temperance School, finishing up at Fleetwood in Nelson County and graduating in 1947.

"A lot of my character that I am today is a product of the elderly farmers I grew up around. They were not educated men, but they had a lot of worldly knowledge. They raised us boys by the motto: be honest, tell the truth, and everything else will fall into place. Another favorite saying was: If you gotta deal with the devil, always deal with one you know! One of my favorites was the one my grandmother told me that dealt with character. She said, 'Son, a good name will follow you for the rest of your life, but a bad one will get there before you do.'

"I'll tell you a story about a tenant farmer named Mr. Angus, who lived on my grandfather's place. He had lost his own farm during the Depression through no fault of his own. I knew the old man pretty good, and he had an old hit-and-miss engine, and I wanted that engine in the worst way. I was working and was making the sum total of eighty-eight cents an hour, and I was going good. I happened to be at his house, and I remember it was in the summertime when the vegetables were coming in.

"Mrs. Angus was cooking a meal and invited me to stay. Back then, it was a flat insult if you were at a home at mealtime, and they asked you to eat, and you refused. During the course of the meal, Mr. Angus said he would sell me the engine. I thanked him and asked him how much? He said twenty dollars. I told him we had a problem, because I didn't have that much money with me. He said it wasn't a problem, and we'd load the engine on my daddy's truck. 'You'll pay me.'

"I had graduated from high school and thought I was a brilliant boy, because I had learned about these notes; thirty-day notes, ninety-day notes, in which to pay off a loan. So I asked the old gentleman if he wanted me to give him a note, and he said, 'No, you'll pay.' I said, 'What guarantee do you have that I will pay you?' You know what that old man told me? He taught me a valuable lesson that day. He said, 'Son, if your word is no good, that piece of paper's not going to be any good either.' And I have lived by that my entire life."

Junior was a good hunter and was about thirteen years of age when he started participating in the sport. As a young boy, he hunted squirrel, rabbit, quail, and deer; when he was older, he began hunting bear.

"Our family had a 1941 Dodge military weapons carrier truck that they put a hard-shelled metal cab on, replacing the cloth top. We would put the bear dogs on the back and drive over to Tye River to pick up Aubrey and Ezra Carr and Carl Coffey, who was a teenage boy at the time, and head up to the Crabtree and into the mountains. I got to know Daniel

Lawhorne, who was the patriarch of the Lawhorne family, and Icem and Clemon Lawhorne, who lived up on Coxes Creek. We all had a great time.

"Icem was the 'driver,' the man who followed the dogs, and the rest of us would get on stands and wait for the dogs to come through. I remember one morning I went up to Icem's house to go hunting, and there was about an inch of snow on the ground. Icem came out wearing a pair of slipper shoes with no socks and was walking around in it with no boots on. He is one tough man.

"One time, I was with the rescue squad up at the head of Coxes Creek where a guy was lost. Daniel and Icem were up there, and someone fired a shot. They looked at each other, and Daniel told us which hollow the shot had come from. Sure enough, they went up there, that's where they found him. We were three miles from that spot, but they knew that mountain like the back of their hand."

Junior's family were active members of the Piney River Baptist Church, where he is still a member. He says that he's a conservative Baptist by heritage, and he has taught Sunday school, been a Sunday-school superintendent, a deacon, and has held every office there is in a church.

"When I was growing up on my grandfather's farm, it was just about as much a law to go to church on Sunday morning as it was to go to the field on Monday morning."

Junior's daughter Karen said that her dad had one pair of overalls to wear for school and one for church. He was baptized in the water from the mill dam at Woodson's Mill in Lowesville.

The mill was owned by Dr. Julian Woodson, but the miller was an older black man by the name of Ed Willis. Junior said that there was always a rumor that Mr. Willis went to work for Dr. Woodson to pay off a three-dollar debt and ended up staying. Junior can remember riding a horse with a sack of corn to be ground slung over the saddle. He said that you could wait for your loose corn to be ground or just make an exchange for meal that had been previously ground.

No money was exchanged because, "we lived by the barter system," but the miller would take a "toll," which was a portion of the corn meal as payment for the grinding service. The amount of the toll was so much per bushel. If there was a lot of grain to be taken to the mill, such as wheat, it would be loaded into a wagon and transported by a team of horses.

Junior's father astride his horse in the 1930s

When Junior was growing up, there were three stores in Lowesville: one owned by Thornton Hite, one by Ward Cash,

Junior cutting Dickie Wood's hair; William Sr. is at far right

and one by the Woodson sisters. These stores were where area families went to make needed purchases.

Junior recalls an incident from his childhood that involved shocking (piling) wheat. "We were shocking wheat with a binder that was pulled by four horses. One man rode the 'wheeler,' which was the wheel horse on the left side that guided the binder through the field. We would walk behind it and pick up the bound wheat and shock it. We had teams of people who would work together putting six or eight bundles to a shock. We'd go back later and stack it until the threshing machine would come by.

"I was wiping sweat and this old fella I was working with had his shirt buttoned up tight around the collar, his sleeves buttoned up, and I said, 'Man, it's hot.' I looked over at him, and he said, 'If you can't stand heat, you better be a good boy, because they tell me it's real hot down there,' as he pointed at the ground. It was the same man who told me about my word being as good as a paper note: Mr. Angus.

"It really bothers me to hear about all this fraud and bankruptcy that's going on now. I've seen cattle sold, apples, corn, wheat . . . you name it, on just a handshake. That's the way they did. Their word was their bond."

Junior said that his grandfather had apples that he sold packed in wooden barrels, three bushels to a barrel. "He grew, sprayed, picked, and hauled the apples to the bottom of a hill for a truck to pick up for ninety-five cents a barrel. Three thousand barrels, holding nine thousand bushels, for less than thirty-three cents a bushel, and yet he made money off of that transaction."

After Junior graduated school in June 1947, he worked on the farm until January 1948, then found work in the lab of the American Cyanamid Corporation in Piney River. His job was to look at the product at certain stages as it came through to make sure it met specifications. Except for the time he spent serving in the army, Junior worked at American Cyanamid from 1948 until the plant closed down in June 1971 because of changing environmental safety standards.

Junior said that if the plant had not closed down, he would have stayed there for the rest of his working life. He said that during the flood of '69, down in the rigging shack where all the tools and equipment were kept, the water rose to seven feet six inches. Junior said that they had everything running again in a record thirty days.

Junior was drafted into the army at twenty-one years of age. He says, "I was twenty-one, single, and in perfect physical condition, so there was nothing to stop me." He was inducted in Richmond and sent to Indiantown Gap, Pennsylvania, where he finished his basic training. He then went to San Antonio, Texas, where he was trained as an infantry medic. When Junior first went into the army, all the boys from the city kept asking the country boys where they went to eat, where they got their food.

Army photo of Junior (1951)

"It finally dawned on me after three days, they were asking what soup kitchen my family went to, to eat our meals. I told them, 'Boys, I'm from the country. I don't have nothing, and I don't know nothing, but I've never been to bed hungry, and I've never slept cold.' Why, I never knew I was poor until I grew up and the government told me."

Junior served in Korea for fourteen months out of the two years he was in the army. "I landed right at the southern tip and went all the way up the peninsula to the thirty-eighth parallel."

As a medic, he was there with the troops on the front lines. He was the first person to get to a wounded soldier. "Those infantry boys watched out for me. I never had to do KP, guard duty . . . none of it. They said, 'You take care of us, and we'll take care of you!' I would bandage them up and get them to an ambulance or helicopter, so they could be taken back to their battalion and on to a hospital."

Junior got his discharge papers on Valentine's Day 1953 and got back to Piney River on March 15. When asked why it took so long to get home, Junior said that he was sent first by ship to Japan, where he had to be processed through, then back to San Francisco, California, to be processed there. He finally got on a plane and was flown to Baltimore, where there was more processing to do before he was sent home.

William Harrison Thompson, Sr. and Jr.

Junior at home with his parents after basic training

"I have no regrets of being in the service other than the two times I did not call or write home to let my family know I was safe; once when a plane had crashed, killing all aboard, and the other after I first got back to the states."

Junior Thompson began his army career as a private but came home a sergeant. He was awarded two bronze stars for military action above and beyond the call of duty.

When Junior was on his way home, he called and asked his parents to pick him up at the bus station in Culpeper. To show how things can change in a few short years, Junior said that he hadn't realized that his father had gotten a new truck and would be picking him up in that instead of the family car they had owned when he left. His mother was now wearing a pair of glasses.

When they rolled up, Junior didn't recognize his dad until he got out of the truck, and Junior saw the familiar striped railroad cap he always wore. He saw someone else inside the car, but it was dark outside, and he couldn't get a good look. Junior spoke briefly to the woman before realizing it was his mother. He said that everything looked a little different after being gone for so long. After he returned he bought his first car, a 1951 Ford. "I've always owned Fords," he said.

When asked how he met his wife, Retha Marie Carr, Junior said that she had finished school at Fleetwood a year after he had, and they had known each other casually through the years. Retha's family operated a store in Piney River. One day, Junior was driving by and saw her in the garden. He thought to himself, "That

Junior with the family car (1953)

William Harrison Thompson, Jr.

Junior with his dad and a new Ford truck

would be a right nice-looking girl if she'd do something with that stringy hair."

About a year or so went by, and Junior and Buzz were still butchering hogs for people in the community, when word came to them that Mrs. Carr had two hogs she wanted killed. The Thompson Twins came to do the job, and Junior began talking with Retha. Soon they began to date. Junior always told everybody, "I killed two hogs for Mrs. Carr, and she paid me off with her daughter!"

Retha was born on February 5, 1930. Both she and Junior were twenty-seven years old when they married on October 11, 1957. The couple tied the knot at Retha's parents' house that evening, and both sets of parents were there as the vows were said.

After a brief honeymoon to Jamestown, the Thompsons returned and lived with Retha's parents until her father died. Their daughter Karen Bettina was

Junior and Retha on their wedding day

born on August 18, 1958, and their second girl, Lori Leigh, came next on August 11, 1961. In 1965, the Thompsons built a house of their own on Route 56 in Piney River, where Junior continues to reside.

Karen's daughter, Kaitlyn Pearce Houchens, was born on January 6, 1996, during one of the worst snowstorms of the year. Kaitlyn is the only grandchild and the apple of the whole family's eye. She is currently a student at the University of Virginia, majoring in English literature. She shares her grandfather's hobby of making things. When Kaitlyn was a child, Junior worked for a year making a rocking horse of laminated oak for his only granddaughter.

Junior showed me two lamps that he'd made for his daughters

A Thompson family portrait

Proud grandpa with granddaughter Kaitlyn

out of push-mower reels and another lamp that has a glass electrical box mounted in the base that actually spins when the light is turned on.

Retha was the perfect doting grandmother, and after Kaitlyn was born, she went to visit her every day until she began walking. Then she'd pack up her granddaughter and bring her home.

In her last few years, Retha had a lot of health problems, and on September 3, 2014, she peacefully slipped away in the comfort of her own home, surrounded by those she loved. The Thompsons had been married for fifty-six years. Junior said that there were very few arguments in all those years.

Unique lamps that Junior made for his daughters

The Thompson household is a multi-generational one that includes Junior; his daughter Karen and her husband, Tim Barrett; granddaughter Kaitlyn when she's home from college; and Junior's youngest daughter, Leigh.

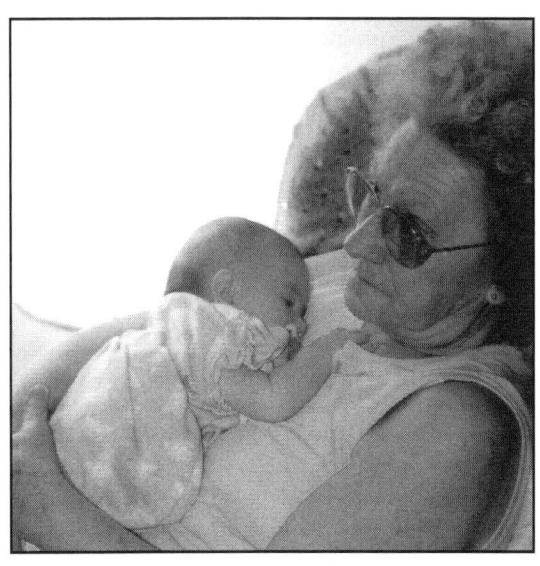

Grandma Retha with newborn Kaitlyn

This arrangement has been the family dynamic for many years because Retha always said, "I want all my chickens in the roost."

Junior said that as the firstborn child of his family, his mother spoiled him; although, each of the Thompson children received their fair share of love and compassion. However, when Junior returned from Korea, his mom amped up her game, and Junior always ate supper with her, even after he was married.

In his parents' house, supper was served between 4:40 and 4:45 p.m. every day, no exceptions. Junior continued this practice even after his dad died. He also said that in her later years, his mother would get on a kick when she'd tell Junior all the things she thought he could have done differently.

On one particular night while he was eating supper, she was fussing at him about something, and Junior jokingly said, "Mama, I am a grown man. I am sixty years old!"

Junior laughed at the memory. "Well, let me tell you, that was the wrong thing to say. I can hear her now, snapping those words off like breaking a stick. 'I know exactly how old you are. I was there the day you were born!' I wanted to laugh so bad, but I knew if I did, it would just get worse, so I just tucked my head and kept eating. She continued, 'And furthermore, I got something else I want to tell you.' I said, 'What's that Mama?' 'I am your mother, and that gives me the right to tell you anything I want to tell you at *any time!*' Mama was the disciplinarian in our family. Yes, I know all about the dogwood switches on my legs. I never got one switching I shouldn't have got, and I should have gotten some I didn't get.

"I got started in the funeral business back around 1969 and 1970, when C. Preston Parr built his funeral home in Roseland and let us use a back room as a station for the rescue squad to house its vehicles. I worked over forty years with the Roseland Rescue Squad, where I was an EMT and a cardiac technician. I am still on the board and do some administration work, but I don't run calls anymore. Back then, we would run calls from Tye

River, Route 664 up by Wintergreen, all around here and down to Arrington, Piney River, Woodson, and over in Amherst County. My famous statement is, 'I've been there and done it. I've seen it all, from births to deaths.' I've literally been on hundreds of calls and that many funerals, taking care of the people, and can say there's not one place that I couldn't go back."

When Preston Parr's health began to fail, the funeral home was sold. Elwood and Marie Byrum bought it in the 1980s, and it became Byrum-Parr Funeral Home. Junior worked part time until Elwood retired in 1993; then Junior became a full-time employee. Many of the mountain people still like to be laid out at home and are buried in graveyards high in the hills of the Blue Ridge, such as the White Rock Cemetery on the North Fork of the Tye River, where it is impossible for the hearse to drive to the grave. Friends and kin people carry the casket of the deceased up the steep incline as they have done for hundreds of years.

Junior said that two of the largest funerals that have been held at the funeral home were for Mrs. Katherine Tolliver, who was buried at Mount Zion Church on Carter's Hill Road, and for a Mrs. Murphy, who was buried at Little Zion on Hubbard's Hill. Ronald Wood, who was a law officer and Nelson County's favorite son, had one of the largest funerals in a church. Ron was Junior's first cousin, and Junior says, "He was a good guy."

When Hurricane Camille ripped through Nelson County in August 1969, Junior said that although they didn't have any damage at their home, which was on higher ground, he was out in the storm from the time the first drops of rain fell until they stopped the next morning.

"I was working at the plant and went outside and saw the clouds. One bank of clouds came one way, and another came from the other direction, and they met just about over the top of Brent's Mountain. It got to raining so hard we had to quit work, and I came home. I heard water running around the house and saw that the rain was filling up the window wells to the basement and were overflowing and starting to come in. I walked around the house all night long, dipping the water out of the window wells.

"When it finally quit, I came up on the porch, and I was so cold, my teeth were chattering. That was the coldest rain I had ever felt. I came in and the power was out, but I got ready to go to work and only made it down to the railroad and the water met us. I had an uncle who lived down by the river, and I went and checked on him, and he made it through. But my brother Buzz was dating a girl in Lovingston and had been down there to see her and got stranded.

"There was a house that had washed down off its foundation, and there were people inside. Buzz went in and rescued three of the people before the landslides came down, crushing the building and washing it away. Buzz and several others in the home were killed that night. The flood happened on the night of August 19th, and his body wasn't found until Labor Day.

"There was one little blind boy Buzz rescued, and he sat him under a tree and told him to stay there, and he'd come get him the next day. They found the boy the next morning, and he was crying. When they asked him what was wrong, he said, 'Buzz never did come back and get me.'"

Buzz lost his life saving others and was considered a true hero by everyone who knew him. Junior worked for five days with the rescue squad, helping to search for survivors and at the grim task of uncovering bodies that were buried in the debris and taking them to the funeral homes.

Junior says he is a true survivor in that he made it through the Depression, he survived the Korean War and Hurricane Camille, and the loss of industry in Nelson County; he's had two operations on each of his eyes; he beat prostate cancer, during which he received forty-three radiation treatments, and a heart attack; yet, he's still here.

He says that there are three things he has a strong dislike for: tobacco, alcohol, and illegal drugs. "I grew up in the middle of moonshining territory and have seen barrels of it and seen it sold for two dollars a gallon. I don't drink it or have anything to do with it. I've seen the effects of it—children going hungry, domestic violence, men's lives ruined."

Junior enjoys woodworking, making all types of picture frames, wooden bowls, and various patterns of cutting boards; he gave me one in the shape of a pig before I left. He said that his great-grandfather, Alfred Wood, was a renowned woodworker in the area, so I guess the hobby was handed down through the generations.

Junior says, "I've always been one to work with my hands. I'm not much for working on things someone else has made. I like to design and make things for myself. I've lived a varied life, a unique life, a good life. When I got ready to leave the army, they asked me where I was going. I told them, back to Piney River. They said, what's there? I told them there might not be much there, but I've never seen nothing I'd trade it for."

Doris Elizabeth Brooks Bryant

14

Doris Elizabeth Brooks Bryant

Doris has always been a favorite of mine. Her quiet, gentle nature has always drawn me to her. Whenever I went into Mount Paran Church, where my husband, Billy, preached, I'd see her sitting in her spot on the last pew with her family and give her a big hug. She'd give me one of her light-up-the-room smiles and squeeze me back. I interviewed her husband, Milton, for *Backroads* newspaper and again for the book, *Plain Folk and Simple Livin'*, as he demonstrated plowing, harrowing, and disking the earth with his enormous black Percheron horses.

The first time I remember seeing Doris was at the Whetstone Ridge Restaurant and Gift Ship at milepost 29 on the Blue Ridge Parkway. Whetstone was a favorite spot for the locals who worked and frequented there. Many Montebello women worked in the kitchen, cooking up huge pots of brown beans, cornbread, and delicious lunches that everyone enjoyed. I don't know how many apple dumplings and bowls of blackberry cobbler I consumed at Whetstone.

While there, I would always talk to familiar folks, asking about families and activities going on in the area. On one occasion, I was in the gift shop, and that's where I first saw Doris. She was running the cash register at the counter. Even though, at the time, I didn't know who she was, I was treated to one of those sweet smiles and cordial "hellos" she is famous for.

The old adage, "Still waters run deep," applies to Doris. She has always been content to stay in the background, letting others go first, as she quietly goes about her own business. That's why interviewing Doris has been such a pleasure. For once, she's the one in the spotlight, telling her life story as only she can tell it. Enjoy this wonderful woman's narrative.

Doris's parents were Marvin William Brooks and Helen Gertrude Hite Brooks. Marvin's parents were William Brooks, whom the kids called "Granddaddy Bill," and Artie Cash Brooks. Helen's parents were Mary and Walter William Hite.

Walter died of tuberculosis while still a young man. Mary died when Doris was around six years of age, but Doris can still remember her coming out to their house, taking Helen's buckwheat griddle out to the ash pile, and cleaning it with the ashes from the stove, making it look brand-new. Wood ashes were gritty, and the acid in them would eat all the seasoning off the griddle. Doris said that her mother would fuss because, after it was cleaned, the buckwheat cakes would stick to it.

Helen's family lived "along South Bottom over from Pkin; across the first set of railroad tracks after the iron bridge." We both laughed when I asked Doris where her father was raised. She replied, "As far as I know, he was on down about three railroad tracks." Helen and Marvin were raised up together and most likely attended the same school, so they were well acquainted when they married years later.

Doris's mother had a daughter, Nadine (born 1932), from a previous relationship. Helen and Marvin had their first child, a son named Coy Leonard, in 1941. The Brookses were living in what was called the Bob Ham house, located on Route 608, when twins, Doris and Donnie, were born on June 11, 1942. Doris said that when her father was going to get the midwife for the birth, someone met him and said, "There's two kids up there, Marvin, and if I be you, I'd catch the number two train and get out of here!"

The Brookses' next child, Walter, was born in 1945; and Sandy, the youngest daughter, came in 1952. The young couple then moved to Steeles Tavern and rented the upstairs of a large white house at the junction of Routes 56 and 11.

Doris grew up near Pkin and stayed there until she married. The area was so small, it didn't have any businesses, just houses where people lived. There were two country stores in Vesuvius, however. Clarence Cash had a store on one side of the railroad tracks, and Edgar Austin had one on the other. Doris said that the family would go up the Coal Road and pick huckleberries (blueberries) and bring them back to sell them to Clarence Cash for fifty cents a gallon.

Doris's mother, half-sister Nadine, Doris and Donnie, and baby Walter

Doris would tell him, "Clarence, you just hold my money." When it came time for school to start, Doris would take her pay as notebooks and other school supplies she needed. While she was talking about picking berries, Doris recalled that one time, her Mama and all the kids were gathering berries, and a man by the name of Duck Fitzgerald, who could not talk, was picking, too. "Duck come out of the woods, making ninety, yelling, 'Barr! Barr!' and Mama saw the bear and said, 'Let's get out of here,' and we turned around and ran after Duck!"

As a child, Doris was never a "girly-girl" and could not understand why her Mama would get on her for not wearing a shirt in the summertime. Doris would tell her, "The boys don't have to wear any," and her mother would say, "I know, but they ain't like you are!"

When asked if her family grew a large garden, Doris said, "Mama tried a garden one time, and she just couldn't do it, so we didn't plant one. Daddy had a good job at DuPont, working shift work, so we didn't have cows or things Mama couldn't do. I didn't know anything about canning or planting a garden until later on, after I got married."

Doris had a playmate named Lou Ellen Phillips, whose family lived close to them. As children, Doris said that they'd walk up and down the railroad tracks and sometimes put pennies on the tracks to see them flatten out after the train ran over them.

"We used to go down to the railroad when the train came and holler at the man in the cab to throw us a book. Sometimes he'd throw us one, and sometimes it would have a candy bar in it. The trains traveled slow then, and we'd walk down to Granddaddy Bill's on the railroad track, and when the train came, we'd jump up and grab onto the ladders on the side as it came by, and ride it back to our crossing and jump off. It's a wonder we hadn't got killed!"

One of the most interesting parts of interviewing the mountain people is finding out all kinds of information you never knew about them. Like mild-mannered Doris jumping on a moving train and riding it home! I had to ask if the conductors ever fussed at them for doing this dangerous stunt, and Doris said that they would get on in the middle of the train where the engineers couldn't see them. "The smoke and stuff from the steam trains back then would hide us," she said.

In earlier years, there had been a school in Pkin, but it had closed by the time Doris was of school age. When she started school, she attended Spottswood, riding the bus that Dick Cox drove. She remembers some of her early teachers: Miss Susie

McCormick, Lyle Humphries, Carrie Lucas, and "Tink" Humphries. Spottswood's elementary grades went up to seventh, and high school consisted of ninth, tenth, eleventh, and twelfth grades. For some reason, many of the schools of that era skipped the eighth grade.

Doris said that she played basketball and went to tournaments, and since she was a tomboy, boys didn't interest her too much at that time. She graduated on June 6, 1961. Then she began attending the dances held at the Raphine Fire Department on Saturday evenings. She met a boy by the name of Milton Bryant, who came to the dances with his cousins, Lemule and Gary Bryant, who all ran together at that time.

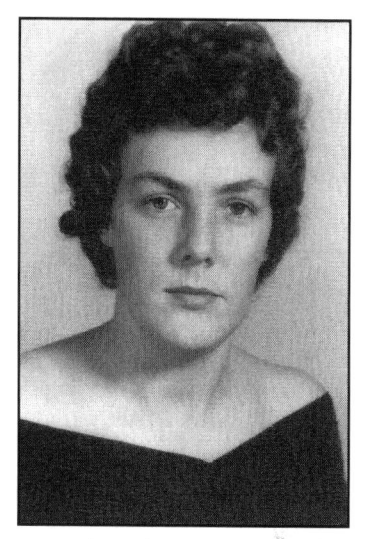

Doris's graduation picture (1961)

As time passed, Doris and Milton began dating; they courted for about a year before marrying. When asked where the couple went on dates, Doris said that they would sometimes go to Hull's Drive-In and watch a movie or go to the Route 11 Truck Stop near Greenville, just to sit and watch the people coming and going.

Doris attended Vesuvius Baptist Church when she was growing up on South Bottom, but once she married and moved to Montebello, she changed to Mount Paran Baptist Church, where she has been a member ever since. The couple were

Milton and Doris before they married

married at Vesuvius Baptist Church on August 25, 1962, by the Rev. Marvin Kerby.

In the newspaper clipping announcing the nuptials, it stated, "The bride wore a street length dress of imported lace over taffeta with a fitted lace bodice. With this, she wore a white hat with nose veil, white accessories, and a red rosebud corsage. Miss Frances Bryant, sister of the bridegroom, was maid of honor; Mr. Donnie Brooks, twin brother of the bride, was best man. Mr. and Mrs. Bryant are making their home with the bridegroom's parents in Montebello, where Mr. Bryant is in business with his father."

Doris said that they stayed with Milton's parents, Melvin and Lois Bryant, from August until Novem-

Wedding day, August 25, 1962: Doris's parents at left; Milton's mother on far right

Mr. and Mrs. Milton Bryant

ber. When Milton found work at the Burlington rug plant in Glasgow, they moved to Buena Vista, renting two rooms from Oscar Hamilton.

Doris had been married for less than two years when her mother died from a heart attack on June 8, 1964, at age fifty. At that time, there were still three children at home: Coy, Donnie, and Sandy. Doris said that her mother had had heart trouble for years, and the doctor had her on heart medicine when it happened. She had been hospitalized several times, and the family had just moved from Raphine to Staunton to be closer to the hospital. From the time they moved there in March, until she died in June, Helen had only spent a total of two weeks in the new house. The rest of the time, she was in the hospital.

Doris said, "She was over at my grandma's, where Daddy's mama lived, and was out in the field picking strawberries when she just keeled over. My youngest sister, Sandy, was with her, and Grandma was sitting on the porch when she saw her fall. Grandma hollered for help, but Mama was gone by the time someone came. The doctor told Daddy not to feel like it was because she was out picking strawberries, because her heart was in such bad condition, it would have happened while she was sitting in a rocking chair on the porch. So I guess she died doing what she wanted to do, which is the best way to go. They buried her on June eleventh, my twenty-second birthday."

Because Sandy was only twelve when her mother

The Bryants with daughter, Deanie

died, Doris and Milton took her in to live with them, and she stayed until she was married. Six years later, Doris's father, Marvin, married Frances Mays. They had a daughter, Linda Jean, who became the second half-sister to the other Brooks siblings.

The Bryants' first child, Darla Dean, "Deanie," was born on February 23, 1963, while they were living in Buena Vista. They stayed there for three more years, before Milton was hired in 1966 as a part-time employee in the maintenance department for the Blue Ridge Parkway. Wilson Grant, who was the supervisor over the Montebello office at that time, was the man who hired Milton.

The Bryants moved to Montebello and lived in a home owned by Wilson and Madeline Grant that was unoccupied at the time. This is when Doris began to live life as a mountain housewife, learning from her husband's mother and sisters how to garden and can the produce raised during the summer, milk cows, and butcher hogs. Doris laughs at the memory and says, "It took a little bit of learnin' to get me going!"

Milton and John Coleman with one of the work horses

Their second child, Steven Alan, was born on March 30, 1966, while they were living in the Grant home.

Since Milton was a part-time employee, he worked six months out of the year and drew unemployment and cut pulpwood the other six months. Wilson Grant and his family came back to Montebello and wanted to move back into the house they owned, so Doris and Milton moved a short distance away to a home rented from Homer Anderson. They stayed about a year before Milton began looking for land on which to build his own house.

Wilfred Mays said that he would sell Milton an acre of land on Fork Mountain, because he was marrying Martha Fitzgerald, and they planned to live farther up Fork Mountain Road. Milton cut all the lumber for a new home, and Floyd Groah framed it up. Elmer Doyle and his sons built it, and in November 1976, the Bryants moved in.

Making a kettle of apple butter

After the family was established in their new home, Milton bought two adjoining pieces of property, and, before he died, Homer Anderson sold Milton sixty-one acres behind Mount Paran Baptist Church, where the Bryants continue to graze forty head of cattle.

For anyone knowing Milton Bryant, his name is synonymous with horses, especially the large black Percheron horses that he has raised and done farm work with nearly his whole life. Doris said that other than the three years they lived in Buena Vista, her husband has always had horses in his barn, sometimes as many as eighteen at one time.

Milton graced the cover of the July 2002 *Backroads* newspaper, in a story entitled "Horsepower on the Family Farm," that showed him working the garden with a team of his massive horses. Although Doris never fooled with the huge animals, she said that she always enjoyed seeing them in the fields, just knowing they were there.

Back in 1968, Doris had decided to go to work at the Whetstone Ridge Restaurant and Gift Shop at milepost 29 on the Blue Ridge Parkway. She did a little bit of everything, from waitressing and cooking to managing and cashiering at the gift shop where I first saw her. It was a perfect job; close to home, with many of her neighbors as co-workers. She recalled one of her co-workers, Alice Humphries of Vesuvius, who loved her job. "They started her out on the counter, taking orders. Then they moved her to the cash register, but when they went to a new kind of computer register, ol' Alice said, 'Just give me a cigar box, and I'll be happy.'"

Milton with one of his Percheron horses

Milton retired from the Parkway in 1999 after thirty and a half years of service. Doris stayed on at Whetstone until the restaurant closed in 2002. The building eventually became the Park Office for the Ridge District of the Blue Ridge Parkway. Doris missed the work and found a job at the Burger King in Raphine, where she's been employed for the last eight years.

Milton passed away on November 30, 2012, after fifty years and three months of marriage. Doris says, "My married life was the happiest time of my life. Oh, we had our ups and downs, and we had our rough spots, but I wouldn't trade them for

Bryant family photo

Brooks family photo

nothing in the world. I'd give anything if I could lay down tonight, and he'd lay down right beside me. I've never had to stay one night by myself since Milton died. My granddaughter

Stephanie stays with me at night, or if she goes somewhere, my grandson Stevie will come and stay. For six months or so after he died, I'd be sitting here about four-thirty in the afternoon and think, well, it's time for Milton to come home."

Kenneth Fitzgerald is Doris's closest neighbor and was Milton's closest friend. Doris says of him, "He was my rock. He went with me every time I had to take Milton to the doctor or the hospital. He was right there with me. He was there through it all, and I don't know what I would have done without him."

Kenneth had lost his wife, Mary, some years earlier, and he told Doris that, over time, the pain of losing your spouse will kind of dull, but you never get over it. Doris says, "Kenneth has been a godsend to everyone on this mountain. Kenneth said every day he thought of something he and Milton did or something Milton said. Milton's death was about as hard on Kenneth as it was on us."

Doris's children, Steve and Deanie, live on either side of her. Deanie has one child, Christopher Curtis Wright, from a previous marriage, and she married Marshall Queen on April 28, 2007. Marshall has four children who were brought to the union. On November 17, 2013, Deanie suffered a stroke, which has incapacitated her at fifty years of age. She receives therapy at home, and Doris says that she prays that God will allow her daughter to regain her speech so she can better communicate with them. Deanie's husband has chosen to stay home with his wife, taking care of her many needs.

Steve married Susan Wagner, and both are employed by the Park Service. Steve stepped into the same maintenance position his father had started out in, and Susan is the administrative technician at the Ridge Office. The couple has three children, Stephanie Elizabeth (20) and twins Steven Alan, Jr. ("Stevie") and Samantha Allison, both seventeen. The twins were premature; Stevie weighed a pound and a half at birth, and Samantha, two and a half pounds. For two tiny infants that the medical profession didn't give a very good chance of surviving, the twins are going strong! Susan also had two sons from before she married Steve, Shawn Thomas Wagner and John Phillip Wagner.

After Doris and I finished talking that cool autumn day, her heartfelt words stuck with me as I drove the Parkway home: "I've had a good life, and I wouldn't trade it for nothing."

Doris and Milton in later years

Loyd Dale Ogden, Sr.

15

Loyd Dale Ogden, Sr.

We first met Loyd and his wife, Lois, at Clemon Lawhorne's homeplace on Coxes Creek when Clem and his wife, Peggy, were hosting their annual pig roast. We immediately felt comfortable around Loyd, who has a warm, engaging personality, as well as a dry wit. We bumped into him time and again at Caul's Service Station near Covesville when Billy and I were out on our weekly paper route delivering the *Bulletin Board* newspaper. Loyd was always in there drinking a soda and talking with the manager, Greg Shifflett, and the locals who frequent the place.

When Loyd's preacher was having some health problems, Loyd recruited Billy to fill the pulpit several times at Shiloh Baptist Church in Faber, where Loyd and Lois attend, and another time to preach a homecoming service. We have enjoyed their company ever since, and I was delighted when they agreed to be part of *Mountain Folk*.

After I had interviewed the Ogdens at their farm, we planned a day trip to the Mount Pleasant community where Loyd had grown up. Billy and I spent a wonderful afternoon roaming the beautiful valley at the base of the mountains, taking photographs for this book. We stopped to visit Loyd's brother Tony and his wife, Wilma, and also made a trip to the

Ogden country store, where Loyd bought me a bottle of turpentine, which is getting harder to find. Turpentine has always been used as a healing agent by the mountain people, and I'm happy to have it in our medicine chest. We had a memorable day, enjoying the Ogdens' hospitality and learning more about this special couple. I think you'll enjoy their stories, too.

Loyd is the youngest of five children born to Oscar Littleton Ogden and Lucy Bet Mays Ogden, who lived in the Mount Pleasant area of Amherst County, which is located at the base of Long Mountain in the shadow of Big Mount Pleasant and Little Mount Pleasant, both of which are sandwiched between Pierce and Panther Mountains.

Big Mount Pleasant and Little Mount Pleasant

The five Ogden siblings, by order of birth, were: Janice Uldine, born on January 10, 1926; Ernest Rayburn came next, on September 21, 1927; Kermit Talmadge arrived on April 26, 1930; Tony Mays on March 29, 1933; and the youngest, Loyd Dale, was born on September 1, 1936.

Loyd's grandparents on his daddy's side were Landon Ogden and Sarah Gordon Ogden, and Landon was one of seven children. Loyd's maternal grandparents were George and Elizabeth Mays, and Loyd's mother, Lucy, was one of twelve children.

Jim, Mathias, and Landon Ogden; George Mays

George owned a lot of land that was passed down to the children as individual farms. Lucy's homeplace still stands, and Loyd remembers it being a two-story, eight-room house with a dining room, a kitchen, a living room that also served as a bedroom, and several other rooms, as well as an upstairs where the children slept. Although at that time the family did not have electricity or indoor plumbing, Loyd and his brother Tony recalled that their mother had a kerosene-powered refrigerator in which perishable foods were kept, and the appliance had the capability of making ice, which was an almost unheard of luxury at the time.

They also had a crank-style telephone, and the brothers remember that their ring was "one long and two shorts." Loyd was just a child when his granddaddy Landon died at home, but he remembers sitting on his uncle Mathias's lap afterward. Landon passed away on December 14, 1941, one week after Pearl Harbor was bombed.

Oscar Ogden with sons Rayburn, Tony, Loyd, and Kermit

Both the Mays and Ogden families were farmers, growing large gardens for home use, as well as all the crops needed to feed themselves and their livestock, such as wheat, corn, and hay. Loyd said that back then, there weren't a lot of insects that bothered the garden plants like there are today. He said that their main cash crop when he was growing up was tobacco, and he says with conviction, "I can't say nothing about people smoking or chewing tobacco, because that was our living."

Loyd explained the exhausting process of what goes into raising a tobacco crop. "It would only take one tablespoon of seed to sow a hundred-yard bed of plants, that's how small the seed was. After the ground was worked up, we'd pile brush on top and burn it to kill any other type of seed that might be in the ground. We'd sow the seed in February and put a canvas over top of it to protect it from the frost after the plants came up. The canvas would be taken off around the end of April or the first of May when the plants were tough enough to withstand the weather.

"When they were about eight inches high, we'd plant them about three foot apart in rows three-foot wide that we plowed with a horse. We had a peg to poke a hole in the ground, put one plant into the hole, and then cover it up with dirt. Back then, you couldn't plant what you wanted; the government told you how much tobacco you could plant on each farm. On our farm, we could only plant one acre. Every so often, they came out to survey your crop, and if you had more than you were allotted, they would pull it up!

"Once the plants were growing good, you had to work it and pull all the grass from around it. You would do this about two times. You also had to watch for tobacco worms and pick them off by hand. If you didn't, the worms would damage the leaves, and you wouldn't get as much money for them. When the plants were so tall, you primed two or three bottom leaves off and topped it, which is pulling the top bud off of it. We would leave the buds on a few of the plants so we would have seed for the next year.

"Each plant would then have about ten or eleven leaves on it. Suckers would grow by the leaves and had to be pinched off about twice before you could harvest the plants sometime in August. We had a tobacco knife to cut the stalks and split them not quite to the bottom. Two men would cut two rows on each side, and you'd be in the middle with a stick, and you'd slide maybe five plants onto a four-foot stick. When the stick was full, you'd lay it on the ground, but you had to be careful if it was real hot, so the sun wouldn't blister it. The sticks would be gathered up and taken to the tobacco barn, where they would be hung on five-tier poles that went all the way up to the top. You could put about five hundred sticks of tobacco in the barn at one time.

"After you left the plants in the barn for a week or two,

A double log tobacco barn on Franklin Creek Road

you'd build a smoke under each rung. You didn't want a hot fire, you just wanted to smoke it good. After the leaves started curing, you'd build a hotter fire under them, and it would take about three to four weeks to finish curing them. What you wanted was a good wet September with cloudy days and a little rain to make it cure good. But if it got too damp, and you didn't keep a fire under it, the leaves would mold."

When Loyd finished telling the work that is involved in raising a crop of tobacco, I remarked about how much time it took.

He laughed as he said, "It takes fourteen months out of the year to raise it! When November come, you take it from the house and put it in a room and stripped the leaves off, and they were put in three or four piles, grading them from bad to good. They were tied up in bundles, eight leaves to a bundle. The bundles were put down in rows on the back of the truck, crisscrossing the rows according to the grade, so we didn't get them mixed up.

"We took them to the tobacco warehouse in Lynchburg to sell, and the bundles were put in big tobacco baskets by grade. We'd spend the night, because if you carried it in that day, it wouldn't be sold until the next day. Auctioneers would sell to the buyers that came to bid on the tobacco, and we'd make a little dab of money. I can remember at that time, if you got twenty-five to thirty-five dollars a hundred pounds, you were doing extra good. For a whole load, you might get two hundred dollars.

"We planted our acre of tobacco, and my uncle was allotted two acres on his farm, so we planted a crop there, too, but we had to pay him a quarter of what it sold for at the market, as his part. In the early days, Daddy used to make the trip to the tobacco warehouse from Amherst to Lynchburg in a horse and wagon."

The Ogden family kept horses for the farm work, cows for milk and butter, chickens for meat and eggs, and they butchered four or five hogs in the fall. They butchered once the weather had turned cold and stayed cold, usually the second week in December. Loyd said that he, his cousin Clayton Mays, and Gordon Tomlin did a lot of butchering throughout the Mount Pleasant community. They got three dollars per animal, butchering as many as eight or ten a day, which Loyd said was good money in the 1950s, especially since gas at that time was twenty-eight cents a gallon.

Although the village did not have a veterinarian, Loyd said, "Mr. Orman Tomlin was our neighbor and was as close to one as you could get. He was one of the finest men in Amherst County. There wasn't many in the Mount Pleasant neighborhood that didn't call on him at one time or another to work on a cow or a horse. If a cow swallowed an apple, and it got stuck in its throat, Mr. Tomlin would take two bricks and hit the apple on each side, so it would go down."

As a young boy, Loyd said that he loved to hunt and fish for native trout in the streams.

"I started hunting when I was about twelve years of age. Why, I'd come home from school and go shoot a squirrel, so we'd have something to eat. Back then, there were squirrels, rabbits, and birds, but around 1950, I started fox hunting with my brother Rayburn and my cousin Clayton Mays. We kept maybe twelve or thirteen foxhounds; Walkers and Trigs, which were the best dogs you could hunt with.

Loyd at ten years of age

"People had chickens, and they would call Clayton and say, 'You all come kill these foxes, they are eating up all our chickens,' which would just suit us. We would follow the dogs on foot up through the mountains. If the dogs run a fox in the ground, we'd dig him out. We'd run a stick down the hole and get him out alive, turn him loose, and let the dogs chase him again. We got smarter by grabbing the fox by the back of the neck and tying a stick to him, so he couldn't get back in the hole. Yes, I've had dogs ever since I was old enough to know what a dog was."

I asked Loyd if he was still hunting, and he said he gave up fox hunting around 1974, after his brother Rayburn died. Whenever he was up in the mountains, it wasn't the same somehow, so he now keeps three beagles and does a lot of rabbit hunting with his longtime friend, Sandy Tucker. "I'd rather hear the dogs running than I would to shoot anyways, just to hear the chase."

Loyd with a couple of his walker hounds

The Ogden family were active members of the Mount Pleasant United Methodist Church, which was established in 1840. One can tell by his speech that Loyd has continued his strong Christian faith throughout his life. The early church was taken down and a new sanctuary was built on the same spot in 1956.

The church cemetery is located across the road from the church, and it is where all of Loyd's family are buried. Loyd said that as a young man, he helped dig many a grave by hand in preparation for a funeral. In earlier times, the family walked the mile and a half to church, because Loyd's parents never drove. They waited until their children were

The Mount Pleasant United Methodist Church

of age and could get vehicles their own. Loyd and his daddy bought their first vehicle, a 1953 Dodge pickup truck, when Loyd was seventeen years old. Then Loyd and his brother Rayburn bought a 1949 Ford logging truck to do that type of work together.

The village of Mount Pleasant consisted of one school, one church, and a country store that was operated first by Mr. Charlie Patterson, then by Hayden Mays.

The Ogden siblings: Tony, Kermit, Rayburn, Janice, and Loyd (1954)

Loyd said that his brother Tony later ran the same store for about two years before building a new one on Route 60 in 1960. At the time, he was also a bookkeeper at the Lynchburg Foundry. Tony worked at the foundry for ten years before he quit to operate his store full time, which he did for fifty-three years.

Tony's stepson, Randy, who had been working for Tony for years, has been operating the store since 2013, after Tony developed health problems. Ogden's Grocery is an old-fashioned country store that sells everything from bib overalls and Wolverine work boots to all kinds of loose garden seeds in wooden bins, tools, and gasoline. It is a game-checking station and has a service garage where Randy does oil changes and state inspections. Loyd says that it is the only store around that never applied for a beer license.

Loyd started at the Mount Pleasant School at six years of age, walking the mile each way through the woods and farmland of his relatives. He attended the first through the third grades,

The Ogden country store in Mount Pleasant

which Miss Nettie Bowles taught, and remembers having to walk close to a mile to his uncle's spring to bring back a bucket of cold water for drinking. The children did not have individual cups back then but drank from a common dipper.

Loyd finished all three years at Mount Pleasant before transferring to the Sandridge School to attend grades four through six. He remembers his teacher as being a Miss Massie. Loyd said, "I had the keys to the school, and William Mays and I would come in early to put slab wood in the potbellied stove to get the fire going before the teacher came in." Loyd finished his schooling at the Temperance School, quitting in the tenth grade when he was fifteen years old to help his daddy cut locust posts with a crosscut saw.

Loyd got his first paying job when he was fourteen; he walked two miles to Clark Campbell's apple orchard at the head of Thrasher's Creek to pick fruit. He worked ten hours a day for twenty-five cents an hour, making his wages two dollars and fifty cents a day, but he could not collect his money until the apple crop was finished. Because of this work, the children didn't start school until much later in the fall. Loyd was serious when he said, "If it weren't for apples, we would have starved to death."

He said that his daddy had a heavy wooden ladder that was leaned against the tree, and he picked from the outside.

The children climbed up the trunk of the tree and picked fruit from the inside. Back then, the trees were full sized, not today's dwarf varieties that make picking much easier. Each person had a bucket at the end of a rope. When the bucket was full, it was lowered down; someone would take it to be emptied and tie another bucket on the rope to be filled.

Some of the early varieties of apples that you don't hear much about any more were the Black Twig, Stayman, Winesap, York, Pippins, Smokehouse, and Grimes Golden.

This was hard, laborious work for men and children alike, but physical work was a way of life back then. Loyd said that he saw his daddy pick apples all day, then come home and cut corn by moonlight. He said, "You'd milk the cows before the sun came up, work all day, then come home and milk again after dark."

When Loyd was sixteen years old and had his driver's license, his next job was driving a wood truck. He and another man would drive to where wood was being cut and load two loads of pulp wood (pine) a day onto his uncle's truck, drive to the Amherst railroad depot, and unload the logs into a boxcar. When I asked if they had a knuckle boom to load the logs with, Loyd smiled and shook his head no. So I asked how the logs were loaded, and he drew up his arms and flexed his muscles.

"They would take logs up to sixteen inches in diameter, down to four inches. Stick by stick, we loaded the logs on the truck by hand, and then unloaded them in a boxcar stick by stick. We got five dollars a day doing that. Daddy had 110 acres, and he, my brothers, and I would cut wood off the land with crosscut saws. Somebody asked me once where I learned to dance flat foot like I do, and I told them I'd cut pine wood and get in a yellow jacket's nest, and if that happened, you could do any kind of step! We skidded the wood out with horses, and we plowed with horses, too. A lot of our land was on the side of a mountain, so we plowed with a hillside plow, going one way, and then flipping the plow over to come back."

Loyd did all kinds of work at home on the family farm. He remembers putting up hay with a pitchfork on his uncle's farm, then taking it to the barn where a large hook would be lowered from the top end of the building. It would grab a bunch of loose hay and pull it up to the loft where it was stored. A horse was used to pull a rope attached to the hook, and if the animal stopped for any reason, they would have to back him up and start the whole process over.

"I also remember helping to thresh wheat when the threshing machines used to come around from farm to farm. All the men came out to help their neighbors, and the ladies would fix dinner for everybody. If there were ten men out there, then ten men would eat. My uncle, Jack Mays, had a hay baler with a motor on it. After the wheat was threshed out, you blew your straw out in big ricks [piles], and we would go around and fork that straw in the baler and bale it. It was hot work, but afterwards we would go over to Mr. Harvey's store near Temperance School and get a Royal Crown Cola for a nickel."

Loyd was twenty years old when he got his first letter from Uncle Sam, telling him to come to Roanoke to be examined. It was almost two years before he heard anything else, but when he did, the military said to be ready to leave. The second time he went to be examined, he was exempted from the draft because of a hearing problem.

In his early years, Loyd didn't date much, but he started going to the dances held on the weekends with his good friend Sandy Tucker and Sandy's cousin, Charles Wilmer. Loyd said that he might take a girl home after the dance, but it was never anything serious until he met his future wife, Lois Marie Mawyer.

"I used to see her standing on the side of the road, waiting for a ride to go to work when I was driving a dump truck for Carlton Mays in 1956. Carlton always told it on me that I said I was going to marry that girl one day." But it wasn't until the next year that he met Lois at a dance at Van Riper's Lake. He asked her to dance, never realizing that she was the same girl he had seen standing on the side of the road the year before.

Lois was the daughter of Aubrey Maze Mawyer and Fannie Mae Drumheller Mawyer, who lived in Covesville. She was the last of five children born to the Mawyers. The firstborn was Andrew, but the infant died just three days after birth. Thelma came next, then Lois's brother Frank. Another brother, Robert, was born before Lois came along on March 21, 1936.

Loyd said of Lois, "I never got to take her home, because she had her own car—a '57 Chevy." They continued to see each other at the Saturday night dances held at the Lovingston Community Center, and Lois finally told him, "If you want to see me anymore, you will have to come after me!"

At that time, Lois had a good job at the People's Bank in Charlottesville, so for many years, Loyd kept the roads hot from his home in Amherst to Lois's home in Covesville. He laughed when he told me, "That's where all my money went."

Loyd and Lois continued to date and went together for six years before marrying on August 17, 1963, at the University of Virginia's chapel. A reception was held

Loyd and Lois before they married (1957)

Lois's parents, Fannie and Aubrey Mawyer (1981)

in the Dominion Room of the Thomas Jefferson Inn.

The Ogdens left for a two-week honeymoon to Myrtle Beach and the Smoky Mountains. They returned to Charlottesville, where they lived on Park Street for three years. In May 1966, they bought the William Purvis farm in Covesville, a beautiful, two-story hilltop home on eighteen acres with a commanding view of the surrounding mountains. They later bought six acres that adjoined their property.

The Ogden newlyweds, August 17, 1963

Loyd and Lois on their wedding day with Loyd's parents

Lois continued to work at the bank, and, by this time, Loyd was driving a delivery truck for Charlottesville Oil Company. He was employed there from 1961 to 1977. From September 1977 until August 1982, he did the same type of work for Exxon, but the company failed and was bought out by Tiger Fuel Company.

Loyd went to work for Tiger at the Charlottesville location, staying until 1994 when they opened another branch in Lovingston. He transferred over to Lovingston, delivering fuel to eight counties in the company's one truck. He retired in 1998 and went back to farming and cutting logs.

The delivery truck that Loyd drove for Tiger Fuel

The Ogdens had been married for fourteen years before their only child, Loyd Dale, Jr., was born on January 12, 1978. Lois said that God was watching out for

Loyd feeding some of his cattle on a cold winter's day

them, knowing that they were getting up in age, so blessing them with a baby. Lois worked to within two weeks of the birth, retiring from work at the bank during the latter part December 1977.

Loyd kept the boy near. He said, "Dale was with me from the time he could stand up and hold onto my neck in the truck

Loyd with a large red oak log he cut in Faber (2003)

seat. He'd fall asleep on my lap, riding with me on the tractor."

Dale married Kathy Diane Campbell, and they have three children: Luke, 10; Nathan, 7; and Tiffany, 4. The family lives a little north of Lovingston, and Dale works for Tiger Fuel. He and his wife also run a sawmill in Dillwyn.

After they were first married, Loyd and Lois attended the Covesville Baptist Church, Lois's home church; in 1967, they began attending Shiloh Baptist Church in Faber, and that's where they continue to be active members today. Loyd is still the best of friends with Sandy Tucker and cousin Charles Wilmer. He says, "Three Amherst boys got three Covesville girls, and all of us have stayed married to the same ones for over fifty years."

In August 2013, the Ogdens were given a surprise fiftieth wedding anniversary party. It was hosted by Velda Zirk and

Kathy and Dale with their three children, Luke, Tiffany, and Nathan

her sister Barbara O'Baugh, whom the Ogdens had met twelve years before at Clark's Ole' Time Music Center in Raphine. They all continue to attend the Friday night dances held there.

Sandy and Charles were enlisted to make sure that the couple got to the Rockfish Fire Department in Afton, where the party was to be held. The men told the Ogdens that they were taking them out to eat to celebrate their anniversary. Loyd said he began to get suspicious when Sandy turned up Route 151 instead of going across the mountain to Waynesboro. Eighty some people were waiting to surprise Loyd and Lois on their special day, and Lois said they really *were* surprised!

Loyd was asked to get up and tell the secret to staying happily married for fifty years. He addressed the crowd by saying, "Well, when Lois and I have a disagreement, I go out on the back porch; and that's where I spend most of my time!" I began to laugh at his remark when Lois chimed in, "Now, Loyd, you *know* that's not right; he is lying again! He never does talk that much, but when they gave him that microphone, he never quit talking, and he wouldn't let me say grunt!"

The Ogdens are still active, going to dances and taking day trips but always coming home at night to sleep in their own bed. Such is the life of a farm family. Loyd has about seven head of cattle that he keeps at home, and he also leases the old James Martin farm in Faber where he keeps thirty head of Angus cattle. They still put in a garden, and quite a few years ago, Loyd grew a sweet potato that topped the scale at six pounds and measured twenty-two inches around! "I carried that potato around for months,

The six-pound sweet potato that Loyd grew in 1995

showing it to everybody, and Lois finally cut it in half and cooked part of it, and it served a whole bunch of people."

As of this writing, there are three surviving Ogden siblings: Janice Coley, Kermit, and Loyd, and they are still a close-knit family. Sadly, Loyd's brother Tony passed away on November 10, 2014, just three days after we had met and talked to him about his growing years in Mount Pleasant. It was an honor to have met this fine man and his loving wife, Wilma.

As we sat at the kitchen table, drinking coffee and eating the snacks that Lois had prepared for us, Loyd summed up the

The Ogden siblings in later years: Tony, Janice Coley, Kermit, and Loyd

interview by saying, "We can't thank God enough for what he's done for us. If it wasn't for him, we wouldn't have nothing."

I, too, thank God for what he's given me, especially the gift of writing, so stories like Loyd's can be preserved as part of Virginia's early history. Many thanks to the Ogdens for their part in *Mountain Folk*, and may God continue to bless you both.

Lois and Loyd at their Covesville farm (November 3, 2014)

Maybell "Mabel" Frances Truslow Napier

16

Maybell "Mabel" Frances Truslow Napier

Although I had never formally met Maybell Napier, who has always gone by the name Mabel, I found that we had an earlier connection. In March 1982, one of my first interviews for *Backroads* newspaper was with Vernon and Clora Truslow, an older couple who lived in Nelson County, Virginia, up a narrow mountain road called Spruce Creek. It turns out that Vernon and Clora were Mabel's parents! How lovely that thirty-three years ago I was interviewing the Truslows, and in 2014, I am sitting down to talk with their ninety-three-year-old daughter.

Adding to the serendipity, we met at Linda Mawyer's home in Afton. I had met Mabel's daughter, Linda, several years ago but had no idea they were related! As they say, it's a small world.

We had a very enjoyable morning, talking and reminiscing about days gone by. I found that Mabel had a strong memory and a sharp wit; she had me in stitches through most of the interview. I thank her for taking the time to be included in *Mountain Folk*.

As an added bonus, Mabel told me a great joke that I'll never forget, and Linda served a delicious dinner after we'd finished talking and taking photographs. The chapter picture shows Mabel surrounded by two quilts that her mother made for her; the one on the left had a note that said, "Gift for 51st birthday, October 2, 1972, from Mama and Daddy," and the one on the right, "From Mama, age 87 years, January 8, 1992." A special thanks to Mabel, and to Linda and her husband, Bobby Mawyer, for opening up their home for the visit.

Mabel's maternal grandparents were Walter Purvis Puckett and Susan Margaret Thompson Puckett, who lived up Stoney Creek in Nelson County, Virginia. Her grandparents on her father's side were Jefferson Napoleon Truslow and Alice Frances Dameron Truslow, who lived a few miles away on Spruce Creek in an area known as Wintergreen.

Mabel's parents, Vernon Shepard Truslow and Clora Belle Constance Puckett Truslow, lived almost at the top of Spruce Creek Road. The Truslows were featured in the May 1982 issue of *Backroads* newspaper as one of the first interviews Bunny Stein and I did outside our immediate area of Love. Several people had said we ought to go talk to the Truslows but warned that we'd have to drive up to their house, because they didn't have a phone.

Mabel's maternal grandparents, Susan Thompson Puckett and Walter Purvis Puckett, shown with Elder Jay Broadhead

I remember the trip up Spruce Creek well. We'd had a cold spring that year, and there was still ice and snow on the ground when we drove Bunny's Volkswagen bus up the rutted mountain road that got narrower and narrower the farther up the mountain we went. We pulled in front of their house, and Bunny said, "I'll stay here and keep the bus running in case we have to leave. You go up and knock on the door to see if they will talk to us."

At that moment, I had the thought that maybe *I* should stay with the bus, and Bunny should be the one going to the door, but I dutifully got out and made my way up the path. The first thing I noticed was the enormous rock on which the house was built. It reminded me of the verse in Matthew 7:24 that talks about a wise man building his house on the firm foundation of a rock.

Mabel's paternal grandparents, Jefferson Napoleon Truslow and Alice Dameron Truslow (August 1920)

Mabel and Linda talked about it, saying, "All of the cousins played on the rock, and Grandma put her fresh-baked pies on top of it to cool. She also spread sliced apple rings on it to dry in the fall. On Sunday afternoons, Grandfather Truslow used to take his hat off and lay his head on it to take a nap on the rock."

Little did I know, until we were invited in and began to talk, that the couple on the other side of the door were perfect examples of godly living. I stepped over a dog sleeping on the porch step and knocked on the door as I watched chickens pecking around the yard. An older man came to the door dressed in bib overalls; he had a sweet smile and the bluest eyes I had ever seen. I timidly asked if he was Mr. Truslow. He

Vernon and Clora Truslow at the house built on a rock

scratched his head and said, "Well I must be, because that's what folks have been calling me for eighty years now."

I looked back at Bunny and waved her in, and we were blessed to spend the morning with two of the kindest people I had ever met. Clora brought out her handmade quilts to show us, and Vernon offered us a glass of cold water from the kitchen spigot; the water ran continuously through a gravity-fed system coming from their spring.

Even in 1982, the Truslows did not have electricity, preferring to have a television that ran off the battery in Vernon's old blue Chevy truck. Mabel said that her parents never did put in electricity for as long as they lived. The Trus-

Mabel's parents, Vernon and Clora Truslow (1982)

lows had grown up together; they walked to school and later fell in love, marrying when Vernon was nineteen and Clora was sixteen. At the time we met them, they had been married for sixty-one years and had six children.

Maybell "Mabel" Frances Truslow was born October 2, 1921. Mabel offered some insight to her name, as she told me, "Dad had a brother who always seemed to have a lot of different girlfriends, so he told my parents to name this baby after his current girlfriend, whose name was Maybell." Charles Joseph came next in May 1925, and an older cousin dubbed the nickname "Jack" on him, and that's what he was known by for the rest of his life. John Wesley was born in 1928, Myrtle McGuffey in 1931, Ollie Lavayer in 1933, and the baby, James Carroll, in 1936.

Clora had all her children at home except Carroll, who was born at UVA Hospital. Mrs. Loving McGann, who was known by her family as "Pretty Mammy," was the midwife in the Wintergreen area at the time and possibly the one who attended the births of the other children.

As firstborn, Mabel did a lot of babysitting of her brothers and sisters. She said that she would walk to visit relatives with her younger siblings and end up carrying them home. Growing up, she helped her father in the cornfield, removing rocks after they had been plowed up in the rows by Vernon's horse. She also hoed dirt up against the plants so that they wouldn't fall over. There was corn in the house garden for the family to eat, but field corn was also grown to feed the animals. Shelled corn was taken down to Grover Harris's mill at the foot of Spruce Creek to be ground into meal that the family consumed.

As children, Mabel and one of her cousins would ride horseback to the mill with a sack of corn to be ground, and Mabel was so little, her Daddy had to help her on the horse. They would take the corn down and exchange it for fresh-ground meal that Grover loaded on the horse; then Mabel would ride the three miles back home with it.

Mabel remembers her daddy making a wooden-wheel wagon for his children to play with. She said, "It would go pretty good down the hill." They would fish in the creek using "pennywinkers," worms they used for bait that could be found around the spring.

Mabel has been a lifelong member of Wintergreen Christian Church, located at the foot of Spruce Creek, and she can remember walking down with her father for Sunday services. Her mother would put whatever coin she had for the church offering in a handkerchief, roll it up in one end, and tie a knot in it so Mabel wouldn't lose it.

When church let out, her father would give her a nickel and let her go across the road to Harris's Store to buy a Milky Way candy bar. On the way back home, Vernon would stop and talk to Alex Hughes and his wife, Sallie (Gene Hughes's grandmother), who would always give Mabel a honey biscuit or something sweet before they left. Mabel said, "One of our ministers, Terry Reister, used to come up on Sunday to preach and come back to the house to visit, and if the meal was on the table, he'd stay a little longer! Sometimes he'd bring his gun along and shoot a little after church."

Like her parents before her, Mabel attended the early Beech Grove School, a three-room building that stood to the left of Cub Creek Road. She remembers, "We walked from Spruce Creek over across Rodes' Mountain on land belonging to Buck Rodes, and there was a path through the woods on other people's property. A man by the name of Raymond Hughes had a big house to the right of the path, and there was a big lake along the way. The path came out on Beech Grove Road. We had to leave fairly early, because it was quite a walk."

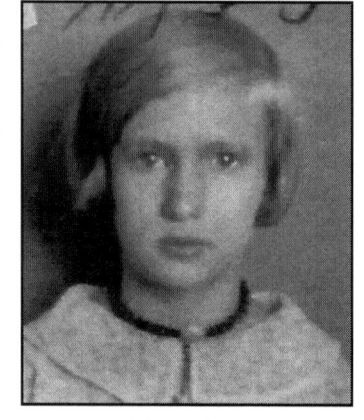

Mabel's Beech Grove School picture (1931)

Mabel's mama packed her lunch, and she carried it in a little metal lunchbox that had two handles. I asked what her mother had packed; she smiled and said, "Whatever was left over from last night's supper . . . biscuits, usually."

Mabel went through the sixth grade at Beech Grove. Helen Norfleet was her first and second grade teacher. Florrie (Harris) Hughes taught third, fourth, and fifth grades. Mabel said, "I loved her. She was so good to me." Mabel's sixth grade teacher was Mr. Jerome Whately, who gave her a gift of *The Little Webster Dictionary*, enclosed in a leather case and inscribed, "Mabel Truslow" on the front page and "From Mr. Whately, December 22, 1933" on the back page. Mabel still has the book.

The Nellysford elementary and high schools

When the school at Beech Grove closed, the children went to the new school that had been built in Nellysford. The state furnished a bus to take the kids to school, and Mabel remembers the bus driver was Cecil Davis. The new school had two buildings; one for the elementary grades and the other for high school. The lower, or "primer," grades were on one side of the elementary building, and Ethel Rodes taught seventh grade on other side of the building.

Mabel remembers that one student in her language class was asked what the meaning of the word "conduct" was. He replied, "I don't know, unless it was a mammy duck."

Mary Moore Hughes taught Mabel in the eighth grade, and Mabel took algebra and Latin from Mr. G. D. Lawman, who later became the principal at the Rockfish School after Nellysford was closed. Linda added that her mother had stopped going to school midway through the ninth grade to help out at home. When Linda and her brother, Roger, went through high school, Mabel studied along with them.

To show what a feisty, self-confident girl she was, Mabel recalled an incident when she had bested a school bully. "When Jack started school, I was a little older, but we had been playing so much at home together that we were really close. I was playing down at the basketball goal and some of the kids came and told me, 'Your brother's crying.'

"I went over to where I knew the other kids would be coming out of the elementary school and found Jack crying because a big boy was picking on him. The boy was bigger than the other children, and some boys were all around him asking when he was going to 'take care of me.' I looked over at him and asked, 'Why are you picking on this boy, and when are you going to stop picking on him?' He said, 'What are you going to do about it?' Well, I jumped up and hit him right in the face, and all the kids started laughing at him. He turned and walked away, and he never did speak to me anymore. And he didn't bother Jack anymore, either! When I started school, I didn't do too bad taking care of myself!

"I remember seeing Dad cut tree limbs with an axe to make some 'tommywalkers,' and I thought, well if he can do that, I can too. The axe went through the wood and into my leg and made a big gash, and I was out of school for a few days." Mabel pulled up her pant leg to show me the scar the wound had left. She said that when it had happened, it bled right much and really scared her.

I had to ask what a "tommywalker" was, and she explained that they were stilts the children walked on. Mabel said, "I could walk wherever I wanted to." I asked if she ever fell off the stilts, and she replied, "I might have, but I knew how to get back on!"

One of the country stores around Spruce Creek was Harris's Store. It had a post office, and people walked down to get their mail. It was also at this store where you went to vote. When Mabel was twenty-one years old and the age to vote, Franklin Delano Roosevelt was president. Mr. "Pal" Thompson, whose given name was Egbert Palestine Thompson, also had a small store up on Stoney Creek that people frequented.

When Mabel's parents were married, Vernon built a log home "beyond the second ford," on the same property where his parents lived. A "ford" is a place where a creek crosses the road; thus, the home was built just past where the creek crossed the road for the second time. In describing the home where she was born, Mabel remembers one big downstairs room where her parents slept, a kitchen, and the upstairs where all the kids slept.

Her Truslow grandparents lived in a house that Vernon and Clora eventually lived in and later bought. "When Grandpa passed away, Granny wanted my dad to move back in the house with her, and she wanted me to sleep with her, which I did until she died. Dad sold the log house to the Napiers, and they took the house down and moved the logs over to Dry Branch, where they owned a lot of land. But the house was never completed, and the family ended up buying a home on Spruce Creek that still stands.

The Napier home on Spruce Creek

"Dad always had horses and also had two mules, by the name of Jack and Joe, that he worked the land with. The creek sometimes would get out of its banks, but never came up to the house. Papa made his own axe handles, whittling them down from wood he cut."

When her parents moved in with Mabel's grandmother, the house was enlarged by adding a new room to the rear. To get to the room, which was used as a bedroom, one had to walk through a hallway where barrels of flour and meal were kept. The children slept upstairs on straw ticks; they would flatten out over the winter and would be refilled with fresh straw when it was cut the next summer. They kept warm, covered with quilts that Clora made, and Mabel recalls that her dad cut shavings with his knife and put them in the stove to get the fire going to keep them warm.

Mabel also remembers, "While we were still living in the log house, Dad kept telling Mama that someone said possums were good to eat. He asked Mama several time to fix it for him, and one evening she fed her and us children our supper first, and then she fixed up that possum for dad because he was late getting home from work. She had it ready for him and on the kitchen table when he came in. He didn't eat a lot of it and finally said, 'Anybody else can eat possum if they want it, but I offered a piece of it to the dog, and the dog wouldn't even eat it! I don't want any more of that stuff.'"

Vernon was a night hunter. He kept coon dogs and would hunt for raccoons. He took Mabel with him, and she said that one time she shot a raccoon. "It was right after supper and Ruler, our dog, had something treed outside. Dad told me, 'Son, get your rifle and a flashlight and go shoot it.' ["Son" was generic for "child" back then.]

"I walked on through the garden and put the flashlight up there and saw the coon out on a limb. I put my rifle up and got it sighted, you know, and shot one time and down came the coon. I told Ruler not to bother it, and I picked it up and took it back to the house. Dad asked what I was going to do with it, and I said I was going to ask a neighbor if he wanted the coon, because he sold the pelts. He came on over and talked a bit before going on home to skin the coon."

Mabel had known Aubrey Owen Napier for a long time, even though he was twenty years older. Owen was born on June 20, 1902. His parents, James Osborne Napier and Missouri Hortense Truslow Napier, built a house farther down Spruce Creek, and Owen was raised there. The Napiers had a large family of sixteen children, nine of whom lived to adulthood.

Owen first found work as a streetcar conductor in Washington, DC, but he decided to come back home when he was older. The families attended Wintergreen Church together, and although there was a big age difference, Mabel and Owen began seeing each other in a different light. As an older teen, Mabel would sometimes ride the school bus because, at that time, walkers were allowed to ride the bus along with the children. When the bus returned to take Mabel home, Owen would wait alongside Spruce Creek Road and wave to her.

Aubrey Owen Napier as a boy

One thing led to another, and the couple began to court. When I asked what her parents had thought about that, Mabel said, "They weren't too happy about it." Owen would ride his horse up the mountain to the Truslow home to see Mabel but always spoke kindly to her parents before leaving. Things got more serious, and it soon became apparent that they were planning to marry.

I asked, "Did your dad and mom let you marry him?" Mabel replied, "They didn't *let*; I did it all on my own!"

Mabel was nineteen and Owen was thirty-nine when they eloped on October 27, 1940. They were married at the Hillsboro Baptist Church in Crozet by the Rev. John Robert Stiff. Here's how it went down. Owen's sister, Sydney, had a car and had already taken Mabel to Lovingston to get a marriage license. The couple went to church that Sunday and were picked up afterward by Sydney, who told Mabel's brother Jack that he'd have to walk home alone, because she was driving them to Crozet to get married. Jack walked the three miles back up the mountain and told his parents what was going on. Jack later told Mabel that when he broke the news, her mama cried.

When the newlyweds returned, Mabel went home to get her clothes, then went back down to the Napiers, where she and Owen lived with his family. When Owen's mother passed away, they continued to stay with "Pappy," as they called him.

After five years of marriage, the Napiers planned for their first child. Linda May Napier was born at Martha Jefferson Hospital on December 10, 1945, delivered by Dr. E. D. Davis of Crozet. Pappy immediately loved Linda, and when she was brought home, he gave up his bedroom to the parents and their newborn daughter, because the room was located next to the kitchen and warmer. He would look after Linda when Mabel had to see about the many chores that required her to be outside.

Mabel returned the favor when Pappy developed cancer on his face, and Mabel carefully dressed his wounds each

Mabel and Owen at her home (July 5, 1942)

"Pappy" Napier, Mabel, and Linda

day. For the last few months of his life, Pappy went to live with his daughter, Lucy, in DC. When he passed away, his body was shipped back home on a train. He was buried in the Napier family cemetery at the homeplace on Spruce Creek. There are four graves in the cemetery: James Osborne Napier, born 1858, died 1948; his wife, Missouri Hortense Truslow Napier, born 1865, died 1941; their two sons, James Samuel Napier, born 1895, died 1940, and Forrest William Napier, born 1909, died 1961.

Pappy died before Mabel and Owen's second child, Roger Owen, was born on June 30, 1949. Mabel had this to say about her son's middle name. "I wanted his middle name to be Aubrey, but there was another girl at church who was pregnant at the same time, and she wanted that name, too." I asked if she'd "stolen" that name, and Mabel explained that the other girl had had her baby first and "yes, she did!"

Clora, Vernon, and grandchildren Lee Thompson, Roger Napier, and Linda Napier (Easter 1950)

The family was musically inclined, and Mabel was playing the guitar by the time she was ten years old. "Dad played a violin and guitar, mom played guitar and auto harp. I was just starting to learn how to play the violin when I took a notion to get married. So that settled that." The music was just in them, and Linda, at age seven, showed signs of musicality, too, and was given piano lessons by Hilda Mae Ashley. At nine years of age, she was playing the piano for the Wintergreen Church congregation, and today she continues to play at the First Baptist Church in Waynesboro, Virginia.

After Linda was born, Mabel went to Waynesboro and filled out an application for a job at what is now known as Wayne Manufacturing. She got the job, leaving Linda at home with her grandfather Napier. Back then, Mr. Pearson Duncan drove a bus to and from Waynesboro, taking people to work and bringing them back home, because not everyone had a car. Owen filled out an application at DuPont on the same day. They called him in for an interview, and the man interviewing him said they'd let him know.

Owen told the man, "Listen, I'm married with a family, and I need this job. If you want me, you hire me today." He was hired that day as a doffer in the acetate spinning department. He retired at sixty-five years of age after twenty-one years of service. After Owen was hired, he told his wife, "May, now that I have this job, why don't you stay at home and take care of Linda and Pappy?"

The Napiers had a huge farm, so Mabel not only took care of the family but ran the business of the farm as well. She sold hay and bartered chickens and eggs at Pal Thompson's store. Linda recalls the day her mother sold a huge load of hay and was walking around the house with fifteen hundred dollars stuffed into the pocket of her apron. This was no small farming operation!

Owen owned all the bottom land, as well as all the land up on Chestnut Ridge—twenty-two hundred acres that joined his brother, Cash Napier's, land. Mabel said, "I had this dog by the name of Two Bits that would walk with me from Spruce Creek all the way over to the farm." She milked twelve to fifteen cows at a time and had a separator to make cream that she sold to a dairy. She saw to it that the chickens and hogs were fed each day, and she spent a lot of time bringing in wood to heat the house and cook with.

Mabel learned to drive when Linda was school age. She learned to drive stick shift in her husband's silver 1949 Willis Jeep, riding the dirt road on Spruce Creek. Linda said that she and her brother, Roger, learned on the same vehicle. They

Napier family photo; Linda at sixteen, Roger at twelve

would be turned loose in the field where there was one rock in the center of the field, and Linda said, "We could always find that rock!"

Linda recalled that her mother raised some baby squirrels whose mother had been killed. "Mom kept the squirrels in a box with a grate on top in the kitchen, so they would keep warm. She fed them milk with a medicine dropper until they were bigger." When it came time to turn them loose, Linda said that they were somewhat domesticated, but they let them go in the big walnut tree by their house. A few days later, there was a terrible racket in the stovepipe. They took the pipe off and out dropped one of the squirrels, covered in soot. They couldn't catch the squirrel, and it ran all through the house making quite a mess before they could get it back outside.

Linda also recalls a story about her dad's sisters visiting from Washington, DC, who wanted some fresh chicken the next time Mabel butchered. A few weeks later, Mabel obliged them by packing up two boxes of slaughtered birds and sending them to the sisters by mail. The sisters waited for about a week and a half, but the packages didn't arrive. When they finally did, the postman carried up the packages and threw them on the porch. By this time they were reeking!

Mabel had better luck shipping eggs to Arlington in a box that held six dozen eggs at a time. She was a hard worker and a bit of an entrepreneur, too. In fact, Linda shared that if her mother wanted some type of furniture that they didn't have, she'd go out and find a piece of board to make it herself. To which Mabel replied, "I did . . . I could kind of get it together!"

I asked who some of the other people living along Spruce Creek were, and Mabel started naming them: "Saylor and Pearl Hatter lived above us, Billy and Gracie Hughes, Vernon and Virgie Hughes. I picked apples for him and Mr. Jhick Davis as a child. Cliff and Eliza Truslow, Sid and Trosy Allen, some Campbells, and Leslie Allen lived across the creek in a two-story log cabin."

I asked about early funerals along Spruce Creek. Mabel said there is a cemetery at Manley Springs near where she grew up, and she remembers being at a child's funeral as a young girl. She recalls that the person conducting the service was Jack Hughes of Nellysford, who was burying his grandson. Mabel said that it was a beautiful service, and she was so impressed by his prayers.

She also remembers when Mrs. Harris died, and her casket was set in the entry hall of the mansion where she lived. The Coleman family had originally built the beautiful home named "Wintergreen" on top of the hill adjacent to Wintergreen Church, and John Will Harris's family lived there after the Colemans left. There is a graveyard on the hill by the house with members of both families buried there, as well as a Revolutionary War soldier. Although the old home is now abandoned, it is still in the Harris family.

Another large home in the area of Elk Hill was always referred to as the Ewing place after the Ewing family who built it. It is now owned by Peter and Betsy Agelasto. Linda said that Pappy Napier worked for the Ewings at one time and bought the homeplace property from Mrs. Ewing back in 1893.

Mabel is one of the few people who can say that she has lived most of her life on the same road she was born and raised on. In fact, Mabel has lived on Spruce Creek so long, she says, "I think they ought to rename it after me!"

Mabel and Owen (October 8, 1976)

Mabel's beloved Owen passed away on September 12, 1984, and is buried in the Rockfish Valley Baptist Church cemetery near Nellysford. After his death, Mabel continued to live by herself at their Spruce Creek home until 2008, when she became a resident of Augusta Nursing and Rehab in Fishersville. Mabel, her sister Ollie, and her brother Carroll are the surviving three siblings of the original six children born to Vernon and Clora Truslow.

Vernon and Clora with their six children: Ollie, Jack, Myrtle, Carroll, Wesley, and Mabel

When the delightful interview came to an end, and I asked if there was anything else she'd like to add to the story, Mabel laughed and replied, "I don't know how there *could* be anything else!" But she made one final comment, "I am thankful to say I've lived a decent life, a respectable life. Growing up, we worked hard, but all in all, we had a good life."

Mabel and her daughter, Linda (September 16, 2014)

For your time, for the rich history of your ninety-three years, I am thankful. May God tenderly keep you in his care, Mabel. You are a treasure!

Annie Ramsey, Zink's Mill School Road

Photo of Back Creek by Vanessa Fraser of Love, Virginia

Back Creek
by Lynn Coffey

Autumn leaves drift silently down
The flowing waters of Back Creek,
Amid tumbling rocks and native trout
Coming from mountains deep.

Bubbling up from underground springs
Below our cabin here in Love,
Converging as one on a downward path
Gaining speed from the freshets above.

Once I lived in a rustic camp
Where the creek split 'round it in two,
Joining together to form a pond
From the porch, a beautiful view.

The water was cold and clear as glass
Unpolluted from man's own hand,
A metal dipper that hung on the spring,
Was used to drink deeply from the land.

The creek wound its way through narrow gaps
Widening out near Sherando's base,
Before emptying into the River South
Bound for the Atlantic with haste.

And so, a little creek can teach us much
About following its path to the sea,
If we, as people, will simply heed
God's plan of what he wants us to be.

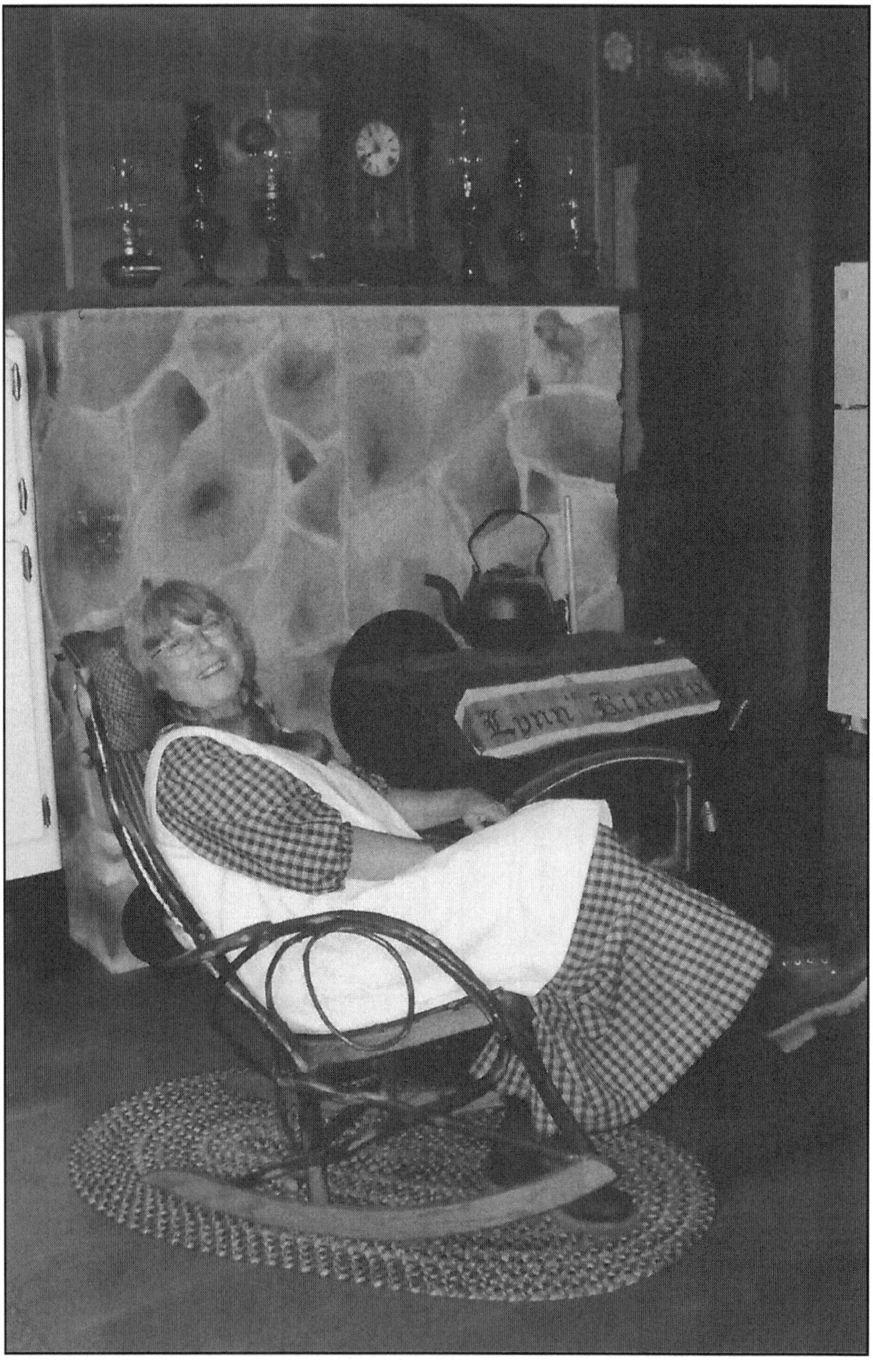

About the Author

Even as a child, Lynn had a Waldenish bent toward a nineteenth-century existence, despite the fact that she was being raised by city parents and growing up along the busy Gold Coast of southern Florida, with all the amenities of modern living. Her dream was to someday build a log cabin in the mountains and live a quiet, self-sufficient lifestyle.

Lynn began living that dream upon moving to the tiny hamlet of Love, Virginia, in the summer of 1980. As she met and got to know her neighbors, all of whom were quite elderly at the time, she soon realized that the culture of these hearty Scottish/Irish descendants was slowly ebbing away and somehow needed to be preserved.

Without any formal education or prior experience in journalism, Lynn carved out a folksy niche, documenting early Appalachian life through the pages of a monthly newspaper that she and her neighbor, Bunny Stein, created called *Backroads*. The first issue was published in December 1981.

Bunny left the after the first year, and Lynn published the newspaper solo for the next twenty-four years. *Backroads* chronicled the early history of the mountain people, and Lynn traveled the hills and hollers to interview the native elders and photograph them, as well as their handicrafts and the activities that had been handed down for generations.

Little did she realize how entwined her life would become with theirs or how much the mountain people would come to mean to her as they opened their hearts to trust a young woman who had started out as a Florida flatlander and ended up becoming one of them.

When she stopped publishing *Backroads* in December 2006, the mountain people's cry, "Don't let our stories die with your retirement," haunted Lynn. She began compiling the articles from the old newspaper and put them into book form. Four books about the Appalachian culture resulted: *Plain Folk and Simple Livin'*, *The Road to Chicken Holler*, *Faces of Appalachia*, and *Appalachian Heart*. This fifth and last book, *Mountain Folk*, is written as a tribute to the gentle mountain people who grew up the old way.

Lynn believes that God has his hand on each individual and has a certain task he wants each to accomplish during the years he gives them on earth. Lynn's advice to the world at large is, "Find your path, and do not stray from it. Walk resolutely toward your goal and don't let anyone discourage you from your dreams. Because . . .

If you do what God has called you to do, in the end, you will be fulfilled, and the world will be blessed."

You can order additional copies of *Mountain Folk* or other books by Lynn Coffey by using this order form.

ORDER FORM

Name _____

Address _____

City, State, Zip _____

Mountain Folk	_____	copies
Appalachian Heart	_____	copies
Backroads	_____	copies
Backroads 2	_____	copies
Backroads 3	_____	copies

The price of each book is $20.00. Please add $5.00 for shipping for each copy ordered. Make checks or money orders payable to Lynn Coffey and mail to:

Lynn Coffey
1461 Love Road
Lyndhurst, VA 22952
www.backroadsbooks.com

Made in the USA
Middletown, DE
05 November 2022